The British Wars

IN THE SAME SERIES

General Editors: Eric J. Evans and P. D. King

LANCASTER PAMPHLETS

The British Wars
1637–1651

Peter Gaunt

London and New York

First published 1997
by Routledge
11 New Fetter Lane, London EC4P 4EE

Simultaneously published in the USA and Canada
by Routledge
29 West 35th Street, New York, NY 10001

© 1997 Peter Gaunt

Typeset in Bembo by Routledge
Printed and bound in Great Britain by
Clays Ltd, St Ives PLC

British Library Cataloguing in Publication Data
A catalogue record for this book is available from the British Library

Library of Congress Cataloguing in Publication Data
Gaunt, Peter.
The British Wars, 1637–1651
(Lancaster Pamphlets).
Includes bibliographical references.
1. Great Britain–History–Civil War, 1642–1649. 2. Great
Britain–History–Charles I, 1625–1649. 3. Great
Britain–History–Commonwealth and Protectorate, 1649–1660.
I. Title. II. Series.
DA415.G38 1997
97–13193
942.06`2–dc21
CIP

ISBN 0–415–12966–4

Contents

Time line

1638	February	National Covenant is signed in Scotland
	November	General assembly of the Scottish church meets in Glasgow
1639		First Bishops' War between England and Scotland
	May	English army gathers around Berwick
	June	English troops march to Kelso but retreat; Scots line the Tweed
		Truce of Berwick
	September	Wentworth visits London to advise Charles
	October	Scottish parliament and general assembly meet
1640	March	Wentworth, Earl of Strafford, briefly returns to Ireland to oversee a meeting of the Irish parliament
	April	Charles's fourth English parliament (the Short Parliament) meets, so ending the Personal Rule
	May	Charles's fourth English parliament (the Short Parliament) is dissolved
	Summer	Scottish parliament reassembles and passes legislation severely curbing the power of the crown in Scotland
	August	Scottish army crosses the Tyne, throws back English troops around Newburn and occupies much of northern England
	October	Treaty of Ripon
	November	Charles's fifth English parliament (the Long Parliament) meets
		Impeachment proceedings begin against Strafford and Laud
		Root and Branch petition attacks episcopacy
1641	February	English Triennial Act is passed
	March	Impeachment proceedings against Strafford begin
		Alleged first Army Plot
	May	Act against the dissolution of the Long Parliament without its own consent is passed
		Strafford is condemned by Act of Attainder and executed
		Alleged second Army Plot

	June	Act declaring that customs duties (tonnage and poundage) could be levied only with parliamentary consent is passed
		Ten Propositions are drawn up by English parliament as the basis for negotiations with the king
	July	Acts abolishing the Courts of star chamber and high commission are passed
	August	Act abolishing Ship Money is passed
		Act limiting the boundaries of royal forests is passed
		Act abolishing knighthood fines is passed
		Charles leaves to visit Scotland and ratify the treaty of London
		Scottish army withdraws from northern England
		Alleged plot, 'the Incident', in Scotland
	October	Irish rebellion
		Charles leaves Scotland
	November	News of Irish rebellion reaches London
		Ormond is appointed by Charles lieutenant-general of forces in Ireland
		Grand Remonstrance passes the Commons by narrow majority
	December	Militia Bill is introduced
1642	January	Charles tries but fails to arrest five MPs
		Charles leaves London
	February	Clerical Disabilities Act is passed
		Impressment Act is passed
		Small English army arrives in Dublin
	March	Militia Bill, having passed both Houses, is issued as Militia Ordinance
	April	Charles tries but fails to seize Hull
		Scottish army begins crossing to Ireland to restore order in Ulster
	May	Irish Catholic leaders meet at Kilkenny; agree confederation of Kilkenny
	June	Nineteen Propositions drawn up by parliament as hardline basis for negotiations with the king
		King and parliament begin raising armies

	July	Charles again tries but fails to seize Hull
		Earl of Essex is appointed commander-in-chief of parliamentarian armies
		Sporadic violence in England as newly raised troops and recruiting agents clash
	August	Charles raises his standard at Nottingham
		English civil war formally begins
	October	Battle of Edgehill, Warwickshire – indecisive
		First confederate general assembly meets at Kilkenny
	November	Charles's march on London is halted at Turnham Green
		Charles retires to Oxford and establishes his HQ there
1643	February	Peace negotiations open in Oxford
	April	Oxford peace negotiations collapse
		King orders Ormond to open negotiations with confederate Irish Catholics
	Summer	Royalist advances in south, Midlands and north of England
	June	Battle of Adwalton Moor, Yorkshire – royalist victory
		Royalists besiege Hull
	July	Battle of Lansdown, Somerset – royalist victory
		Battle of Roundway Down, Wiltshire – royalist victory
		Royalists take Bristol
		Westminster Assembly begins meeting to discuss future religious settlement of England and Wales
	August	Royalists besiege Gloucester
	September	Parliamentarians relieve Gloucester
		First battle of Newbury, Berkshire – indecisive
		Charles I concludes a truce with the confederate Irish Catholics
		Parliament concludes an alliance with the Scots
	October	Battle of Winceby, Lincolnshire – parliamentarian victory

	November	King appoints Ormond lord lieutenant of Ireland
	December	Death of John Pym
		Troops from Ireland land near Chester to fight for the king in England
1644	January	Scottish army enters England to fight for parliament
		The royalists' alternative 'parliament' meets in Oxford
		Parliament's Executive Committee of Both Houses expanded to include Scots and renamed the Committee of Both Kingdoms
		Battle of Nantwich, Cheshire – parliamentarian victory
	March	Parliamentarian army is mauled and captured outside Newark, Nottinghamshire
		Battle of Cheriton, Hampshire – parliamentarian victory
	April	Scottish and English parliamentary armies converge on York to lay siege to the royalists' northern capital
	June	Battle of Cropredy Bridge, Oxfordshire – royalist victory
		York tightly besieged
		Prince Rupert leads royalist army north to relieve siege of York
	July	Battle of Marston Moor, Yorkshire – parliamentarian victory
		Inchiquin declares for parliament and resumes hostilities against the confederate Irish Catholic forces in Munster
		Antrim's Irish forces, under MacDonald, land in western Scotland
		Parliamentarians take York
	August	Essex leads parliamentarian army into the south-west
		Essex's army is mauled around Lostwithiel, Cornwall
	September	Essex's army surrenders at Fowey, Cornwall
		Battle of Tippermuir, near Perth – Montrose defeats covenanter forces

	October	Second battle of Newbury, Berkshire – indecisive, despite parliamentarian advantages
	November	Performance of parliamentarian armies and senior officers strongly criticised in parliament
	December	Self-Denying Ordinance is introduced in parliament
1645	January	Archbishop Laud is executed
		Peace negotiations open in Uxbridge
		Parliament begins considering recommendations of Westminster Assembly; approves a new Directory of Worship
	February	Battle of Inverlochy – Montrose defeats covenanter forces
		Ordinance is passed to reorganise parliamentarian forces and establish a new model army
		Uxbridge peace negotiations collapse
	April	Self-Denying Ordinance passed
		Sir Thomas Fairfax replaces Essex as commander-in-chief of the parliamentarian armies; many other senior officers are replaced
	May	Battle of Auldearn, near Nairn – Montrose defeats covenanter forces
		Royalists capture and sack Leicester
	June	Battle of Naseby, Northamptonshire – parliamentarian victory
		Earl of Glamorgan arrives in Ireland
	July	Battle of Alford – Montrose defeats covenanter forces
		Battle of Langport, Somerset – parliamentarian victory
		Parliamentarian armies begin mopping up remaining royalist pockets in Midlands, south-west and Wales
	August	Parliament begins making provision to establish presbyterian-type churches in England and Wales
		Battle of Kilsyth – Montrose defeats covenanter forces

		Glamorgan reaches a secret deal with the confederate Irish Catholics
	September	Parliamentarians take Bristol
		Battle of Philiphaugh, near Selkirk – Montrose defeated by covenanter forces
		Battle of Rowton Moor, Cheshire – parliamentarian victory
	October	Major royalist stronghold of Basing House, Hampshire, is stormed and captured by parliamentarians
		Rinuccini arrives in Ireland
	December	Secret deal between Glamorgan and the confederate Irish Catholics is revealed; it is repudiated by the king and Glamorgan is briefly imprisoned
1646	February	Parliamentarians take Chester
		Battle of Torrington, Devon – parliamentarian victory
		Ordinance abolishing the Court of Wards is passed
	March	Further Ordinances are passed to set up presbyterian churches in England and Wales
		Royalist army in the south-west surrenders near Truro, Cornwall
	Spring	Negotiations between Ormond and confederate Irish Catholics
	April	English parliament appoints Viscount Lisle lord lieutenant of Ireland
	May	Charles surrenders to the Scottish army besieging Newark, Nottinghamshire
		Royalist Newark surrenders
	June	Battle of Benburb, County Tyrone – confederate Irish forces defeat the Scottish Ulster army
		Royalist Oxford surrenders
		Effective end of the civil war of 1642–6
	July	Parliament draws up Propositions of Newcastle as basis for settlement with the defeated king
	August	Rinuccini renounces proposed confederate

		London; radicals present the Agreement of the People
		Battle of Knocknanuss, near Mallow – Inchiquin defeats confederate Irish Catholic army
	November	Putney debates ended
		Charles escapes from Hampton Court
		Charles in renewed captivity at Carisbrooke Castle, Isle of Wight
		Army mutiny at Ware, Hertfordshire, is crushed and order restored
	December	Charles concludes an alliance with the Scots
1648	January	Parliament breaks off negotiations with Charles
	March	Anti-parliamentarian rising in south Wales
	April	Riot in Norwich, Norfolk
		Hardening attitude towards Charles in parliamentarian army
		Border towns of Berwick and Carlisle fall to English royalists
	May	Welsh royalists are defeated at St Fagan's, Glamorganshire, and retreat into Pembrokeshire
		Royalist rising in Kent
		Truce between Inchiquin and the confederate Irish Catholics
	June	Parliamentarian forces under Fairfax capture Maidstone, Kent
		Kentish royalists cross into Essex and occupy Colchester
		Fairfax besieges rebel-held Colchester
		Cromwell besieges rebel-held Pembroke
		Sporadic riots and minor risings in other parts of England and Wales
	July	Cromwell takes Pembroke
		Scottish-royalist army enters England
		Cromwell marches north to engage Scottish-royalist army of invasion
	August	Battle of Preston, Lancashire – Cromwell defeats the Scottish-royalist army
		Fairfax takes Colchester

	September	Parliament reopens negotiations with Charles at Newport, Isle of Wight
		Ormond returns to Ireland
		Anti-royalist covenanters regain control of Scottish government
	October	Cromwell visits Scotland
	November	Growing army discontent at parliament's willingness to reach a deal with Charles; army moves closer to London
	December	Army enters London
		Army purges the House of Commons
		Preparations for the trial of the king
		Charles brought to London
1649	January	Purged House of Commons authorises the trial of the king
		Ormond concludes treaty with confederate Irish Catholics
		Charles tried and executed
	February	House of Commons resolves to abolish monarchy in England, Wales and Ireland and to abolish the House of Lords
		Scots proclaim Charles, Prince of Wales, king of Great Britain and Ireland
		Rinuccini leaves Ireland
	March	Acts passed to abolish monarchy and House of Lords
	May	Army mutiny crushed at Burford, Oxfordshire
		Act declaring England to be a free Commonwealth is passed
	June	Forces of Irish-royalist alliance capture territory and threaten Dublin
	August	Battle of Rathmines – Irish-royalist army defeated by English parliamentarian forces under Michael Jones
		Part of the English army under Cromwell sent to restore English control of Ireland
	September	Cromwell captures Drogheda
	October	Cromwell captures Wexford and New Ross
	November	Death of Owen Roe O'Neill

		Cromwell captures Carrick and besieges Waterford
1650	February	Cromwell captures Fethard and Cahir
	March	Cromwell captures Kilkenny
	April	Montrose's pro-royalist campaign in northern Scotland ends with defeat at Carbisdale
	May	Montrose is executed
		Cromwell captures Clonmel
		Cromwell leaves Ireland; is replaced by Henry Ireton
	June	Fairfax resigns; Cromwell becomes commander-in-chief of the parliamentarian army
		Charles II takes the covenants in order to secure Scottish support
		Battle of Scarrifhollis, near Letterkenny – parliamentarian forces defeat native Irish Ulster army
	July	Part of the English army under Cromwell launches an invasion of Scotland
	August	Charles II repudiates Ormond's treaty with the confederate Irish Catholics in order to confirm Scottish support
	September	Battle of Dunbar – Cromwell defeats Scottish-royalist army
		Cromwell enters Edinburgh
	October	Some covenanters issue a remonstrance opposing Scottish support for the king
		Cromwell enters Glasgow
	November	Covenanter forces of south-west Scotland are defeated outside Hamilton
	December	Pro-royalist covenanters issue a resolution to allow old royalists to serve in the Scottish army; strict covenanters protest
1651	January	Charles II crowned at Scone
	July	Battle of Inverkeithing – part of Cromwell's army defeats part of the Scottish-royalist army
		Much of Cromwell's army crosses the Firth of Forth

	August	Scottish-royalist army enters England, reaches Worcester and is surrounded there
	September	Battle of Worcester – parliamentarian victory effectively ends the series of internal British wars
	October	Limerick falls to Ireton after a long siege
	November	Death of Henry Ireton
1652	April	Galway falls to English troops
	August	Act for the Settlement of Ireland is passed
1654	April	Ordinance for the Union of England and Scotland is passed

Map 1 England and Wales, 1639–51

Carbisdale

Auldearn

Alford   Aberdeen

Inverlochy

Scone
Tippermuir   Perth

Stirling   Inverkeithing

Dunbar
Kilsyth

Glasgow   Edinburgh   Kelso

Hamilton   Berwick

Philiphaugh

0	50	100	150 km
0		50	100 miles

Map 2 Scotland, 1639–51

xxiii

Londonderry

ULSTER

Benburb

Newry

Dundalk

Drogheda

Trim

Dungan Hill

Dublin

Rathmines

CONNACHT

Galway

LEINSTER

Scarrifhollis

Kilkenny

Limerick

Cashel
Cahir

Fethard

New Ross

Clonmel

MUNSTER

Carrick

Wexford

Knocknanuss

Dungarvan

Cork

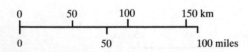
Map 3 Ireland, 1641–52

1

Introduction: an English or a British civil war?

In the early 1640s England and Wales were gripped by a political and religious crisis, triggered by the actions of King Charles I, though underlain by broader and longer-term issues. The crisis came to dominate central government, but it was not contained there. Instead, during 1642 deeper, armed divisions were engendered, spilling over into war. For the following four years England and Wales were engulfed by civil war between the forces of king and parliament. Much of the country witnessed bloodshed, and even those parts spared direct military conflict endured heavy, repeated demands imposed by a national civil war. Although in 1646 parliament completed a decisive military victory over the king, so ending the principal or first civil war, many of the problems which had caused the war remained unresolved and others had arisen as divisions opened up, even within the parliamentary cause itself, in the course of fighting a long war. The king's refusal firmly to commit himself to a political settlement which commanded the support of most of the power groups emerging from the civil war wrecked the constitutional negotiations of 1646–7, and his actions encouraged a return to violence during 1648. That year was marked by risings in many parts of England and Wales, some pro-royalist, others anti-parliamentarian, collectively labelled the second civil war. The victory of parliamentary forces in this renewed war led on to the forcible restructuring of government during winter 1648–9, including the purging of the House of Commons, the trial and execution of the king, the abolition of monarchy and the House of Lords, and the establishment of a new republican government.

1

A decade of unprecedented political crisis, civil war and constitutional uncertainty in England and Wales had profoundly affected politics, government, religion, the church, the political and intellectual climate, and the people of England and Wales.

It is impossible, however, fully to understand these developments in England and Wales without appreciating the role of Scotland and Ireland, whose histories had long intertwined with those of their near neighbours. From 1603 they shared a single monarch, and the king who fought and lost the civil war in England and Wales was also king of Scotland and Ireland. The causes, course and consequences of the civil war in England and Wales involved and in part depended upon Scottish and Irish factors. Scotland precipitated the crisis of the early 1640s by successfully rising against royal policies in the late 1630s and by defeating the king's attempt to quell and conquer it. Until he concluded peace with the Scots in summer 1641, the king remained extremely vulnerable and was almost powerless in England during 1640–1. In autumn 1641 the rising of Irish Catholics brought into urgent focus remaining areas of disagreement between the king and his English parliament, helped to widen the conflict and to destroy remaining trust and so contributed to the slide into war in England and Wales. During the civil war of 1642–6 both sides looked to Scotland and Ireland for assistance. The king attempted to make deals with various factions in Ireland in order to bring troops over to fight for him in England and Wales. With rather more success, parliament made an alliance with the Scots which brought in Scottish troops to fight in England and Wales. This direct Scottish intervention contributed significantly to the military victory of 1646, but the tensions caused by the wartime Scottish and Irish alliances also contributed to the failure to reach a settlement after it. The most potent threat to the English parliament during the renewed civil war of 1648 was the arrival on English soil of a pro-royalist Scottish army of invasion. Once the renewed royalist threat in England and Wales, including this Scottish army, had been crushed, the restructured English government and its army set about extending its authority over both Scotland and Ireland. Military campaigns, largely successful, were conducted in both kingdoms. They resulted in a degree of English control over, and political incorporation of, Scotland and Ireland more ambitious and effective than anything that had gone before.

This Scottish and Irish dimension to developments in England and Wales has long been recognised and is found in most traditional accounts of what has often been labelled the English civil war. Within the last generation, however, this approach to the mid-seventeenth-century wars in England and Wales has been challenged and in part superseded by the recent fashion for studying '(New) British History'. Emerging in the 1980s, it emphasises the need to study the histories of England, Wales, Scotland and Ireland as parts of a single process, and suggests that only in this way is it possible fully to understand the complex interrelationships between the various peoples and component kingdoms of the British Isles. Historians of the seventeenth century who have pursued this new line – including, to varying degrees, John Pocock, John Morrill and Conrad Russell – are often critical of a coverage of Scotland and Ireland which portrays them merely as contributory factors to the outbreak of the English civil war and as bit players occasionally caught up in the English conflict and unintentionally affected by it. Instead, there has arisen a greater awareness of the depth and importance of Scottish and Irish factors and a greater willingness to explore more fully and sharply the British aspects of the events of the mid-seventeenth century.

Much of this new work has focused on the outbreak of the conflict. Within the three years 1639–42, large numbers of people in all three of Charles I's kingdoms rose in open, armed resistance to aspects of his rule. This has led to suggestions that common factors may have been at work in all three kingdoms and that the same issues may have precipitated, or at least made a substantial contribution to, the outbreak of war against the king's government in all three. Moreover, it has also been suggested that a situation in which a single monarch attempted to rule several disparate and physically diverse kingdoms – a so-called 'multiple kingdom' – might itself have created difficulties and dangers and so have contributed to the outbreak of rebellion and civil war. Accordingly, rather than listing Scottish and Irish factors among an array of causes of the English civil war, some interpretations now present the difficulties inherent within a 'multiple kingdom' or 'the British problem' as the major factor explaining the outbreak of hostilities in all three of Charles I's kingdoms. Such an approach requires a more balanced coverage of developments in each kingdom in order fully to understand both the conflicts and coalitions within and between them and the causes and nature of 'the British wars' or 'the war(s) of the three kingdoms'.

Although this British dimension has been seen at its fullest in studies of the causes of the conflict, there has also emerged a greater awareness of the direct and indirect influence which Scotland, Ireland, and England and Wales exerted upon each other throughout the rest of the 1640s. Although many assessments of the years after 1642 have retained an English focus, much recent work – by David Stevenson, Keith Brown, Jane Ohlmeyer, Michael Perceval-Maxwell and others – has explored in detail the internal political and military history of Scotland and Ireland, has analysed the relationship between them, and has led to a fuller understanding of, and a heavier stress upon, the ways in which Scotland and Ireland affected and were affected by the course and consequences of the war in England and Wales. The picture emerging is of three kingdoms intimately and repeatedly intertwining, and of a series of political and military conflicts fought out from the late 1630s to the early 1650s which can only fully be understood if analysed within this British context.

However, this new picture must be treated with some caution. From the mid-seventeenth century onwards, the quest to explain the causes of the English civil war and, more broadly, the essence and consequences of the events which rocked all three Stuart kingdoms in the 1640s, has produced an array of different explanations. The historiography of this period suggests that a particular approach may find favour for a generation or two before being discarded entirely or partly incorporated into an accepted foundation upon which the next generation of historians builds a new edifice, focusing upon a new theme. The field is littered with the corpses of once fashionable interpretations, including explanations stressing political, constitutional, religious, social, economic or cultural problems, from which nutrients commanding wide acceptance have been sucked and synthesised. The current fashion for focusing upon the British context may well fade in time. Even now there are sceptics, for example David Cannadine, Nicholas Canny and Keith Brown. Certainly, a British approach runs the danger of ignoring or under-playing both internal factors unique to each of the three kingdoms and the unequal relationship between them. Moreover, it is unlikely to provide a complete picture of what occurred in each kingdom. For example, the contributions of Scotland and Ireland help to explain the divisions within English central government in 1641–2, but probably tell us little about the forces which motivated large numbers of Englishmen and Welshmen in towns and the countryside to take up arms for king or parliament in 1642–3. A three kingdom approach may give us a fuller and more accurate picture of this period, but it is unlikely to answer every question, to convince every historian or to command the field for evermore.

This brief study attempts concisely to explore the paths of all three kingdoms during a period when open conflict, both within each kingdom and between two or more of them, seemed to dominate the course of events. Chapter 2 sets the context by exploring the nature of the three kingdoms and the potential for conflict, especially in the early seventeenth

4

century when they acquired a single monarch. The bulk of this study (Chapters 3–5) focuses on the period from 1637, when large parts of Scotland flared up into open resistance to royal government, until 1651, when English military control over Scotland and Ireland had been fairly well established and when the great campaigns of Oliver Cromwell in both countries were completed by his crushing victory at Worcester over the final attempt by either a Scottish or an Irish army to overwhelm the new English regime by military invasion. Finally, a concluding chapter seeks to pull these themes together and to assess how far the wars of the mid-seventeenth century can be seen as truly 'British' and how far we should continue to see them as a series of interrelated but separate conflicts, involving distinctive English and Welsh, Irish and Scottish factors.

2

Prelude to conflict?: the early Stuart inheritance

Introduction: the problem of ruling three kingdoms

It is far easier to write the history of a single nation than to take a holistic approach to the islands which lie off the north-western corner of mainland Europe and to attempt to present a full, balanced history of the area referred to variously as 'Britain', 'the British Isles', 'Britain and Ireland' or, more lyrically, 'the Atlantic archipelago'. Their interrelating histories are particularly complex during the early modern period. In the course of the sixteenth and seventeenth centuries, the four British nations repeatedly clashed, as one of them (England) completed the political and administrative absorption of its western neighbour (Wales), sought to dominate a second kingdom across the sea (Ireland) and maintained often uneasy relations with the third kingdom on its northern border (Scotland). Moreover, throughout the period the English monarch claimed to rule Wales and Ireland, for most of the sixteenth century the monarchs of England and Scotland were related, and from the early seventeenth century England and Scotland shared the same monarch. From 1603 the Stuarts ruled the four disparate nations of the Atlantic archipelago.

Such a situation was not unique in the early modern world. Several continental monarchs ruled over an amalgam of territories which remained, or recently had been, kingdoms or independent nations in their own right. For example, the early modern Spanish monarchs ruled over a far-flung set of territories, including (at various times) Castile,

6

Aragon, Navarre, Catalonia, Portugal, Sardinia, Sicily, Naples and the Spanish Netherlands. Analysis of multiple kingdoms has led historians such as J.H. Elliott to suggest that several problems might result. Most obviously, there was an absentee monarch. A monarch's selection of ministers might provoke jealousies and antagonisms among the component territories. Each territory might have its own foreign, commercial and colonial interests, conflicting with those of its brother territories, a source of indignation should the monarch attempt to impose a single policy which cut across territorial interests. Similarly, the imposition of financial exactions throughout a multiple kingdom might give rise to resentment, as each territory squabbled about its share of the burden or complained that its resources were being used to further the interests of another nation; such disputes might intensify in wartime, enflamed by increased financial burdens and divergences over war aims. Above all, in the generations after Europe had been rent asunder by the Reformation and conflict between those holding different Christian faiths, religious differences within and between members of a multiple kingdom and any attempt by the monarch to impose a common faith throughout his territories might provoke extremely bitter conflict. Once a dispute had broken out it could easily spread, for other nations within the multiple kingdom might share common interests with one of the disputants or might seize the opportunity to pursue their own goals. All these potentials for conflict lurked within the early modern Atlantic archipelago.

The Atlantic archipelago

England was by far the most powerful, populous and prosperous of the British kingdoms. A vibrant, expansive commercial power, with a large and rapidly expanding population – approaching five million in the years before the civil war – early modern England appeared to be stable, strong and united. It possessed a single system of local government and administration, a largely unified judicial system and, with the minor exception of some Cornish, a single language of everyday speech. Many people at all levels of society took a keen interest in their own county or locality, and those areas far distant from the capital were seen by some as 'dark corners' of the land and, in the case of the Welsh borderlands and the far north, were partly administered by regional bodies. However, by the seventeenth century England was a united and centralised state, well ordered and generally peaceful. It had shown itself able to survive the religious upheavals and dynastic uncertainties of the Tudor age without major dislocation.

7

England was ruled by an hereditary monarchy possessing extensive royal powers, including the right to make peace and war, appoint and dismiss officers of state, and call, prorogue and dissolve parliaments. The monarch was the font of all justice and commander-in-chief of all armed forces. Although he could not make new laws or impose new taxes alone, he had at his disposal an array of existing statutes and precedents which could be revived, and might also take on enhanced powers during wars or other emergencies. The crown headed a well-established system of central government, comprising the executive – principally the king's privy council – the legislature – a parliament of two houses, one of hereditary peers and bishops, the other of elected representatives of the nation – and the judiciary. Some elements of central government were under strain by the seventeenth century, especially the essentially medieval system of state finance, which was failing efficiently to tap the wealth of the nation and was increasingly reducing the monarch and his government to penny-pinching in peacetime and desperation in wartime. In general, however, English central government had performed adequately under the Tudors.

Throughout the Middle Ages, the English crown had claimed authority over parts or all of Wales and had mounted intermittent military campaigns against the native celtic Welsh. The process of conquest, colonisation and assimilation had been largely completed by the sixteenth century and the Tudors rounded it off through a formal union. Between 1536 and 1543 Acts of Union extended English justice and administration throughout Wales and the borders and granted Welsh shires representation in the English House of Commons, underlining the political and constitutional union. A separate Welsh racial and cultural identity survived, as did a distinctive Welsh language, though it had ceased to be the language of justice and administration. However, in terms of government, politics and religion, Wales was effectively united to, and assimilated within, England. Although historians are now acutely aware of the distinctive contributions of Scotland and Ireland to the mid-seventeenth-century crises, it is hard to discern a distinctive Welsh role which is not mirrored in parts of England. Wales and the 400,000 Welsh could not escape the political turmoil and conflict of the period and they made an important contribution to the civil wars. But there is no particular and exclusively Welsh role within either the English or the British wars.

Early modern Ireland was riddled with potential fracture lines. Its medieval history was as a divided territory over which English kings had claimed powers of overlordship and had exerted a degree of political control through conquest and diplomacy. English authority had waned during the later Middle Ages, but from the 1530s the Tudors had re-established direct English control. They had been helped by the racial and political cleavages within the Irish population, for the million or more people who lived in early modern Ireland fell into a number of different historical groupings. The oldest group were the native, gaelic Irish, sometimes referred to as the 'old Irish', who were the descendants of the pre-Norman inhabitants of the island. From the Norman conquest to the fifteenth century, large numbers of people had moved across from the British mainland and had settled in Ireland. Referred to variously as the 'Anglo-Irish', the 'old English' or, occasionally, the 'new Irish', they were descended from peoples who at one time lived in England, Scotland, Wales or Normandy, but by the early modern period most had deep roots in Ireland. Some, however, retained the distinctive characteristics of their origins, particularly an enclave of gaelic Scots who had settled in the north-east corner of the island and who maintained close links with their kinsfolk of the western highlands and islands of Scotland; for them, the North Channel was a highway, linking the two halves of this Scottish gaelic community. The sixteenth century had seen a new wave of principally English colonisers, riding on the back of renewed English dominance of Ireland, and generally referred to as the 'new English'; increasingly, this group monopolised office-holding at the centre and by the early seventeenth century dominated the English government of Ireland. To add to this racial and cultural mix, the opening decades of the seventeenth century saw another wave of colonists, most of them drawn from the Scottish lowlands and settling particularly in the north, in the province of Ulster.

The English political elite tended to view early modern Ireland as a conquered nation, a colonial kingdom subordinate to the English crown, its peoples to be governed and its land colonised as the English government saw fit. In 1541 the English crown and parliament declared that Ireland was a kingdom and that the king of England was also to hold the Irish crown. There was a devolved royal government of sorts in Ireland, based in Dublin, comprising a governor – holding the title lord lieutenant or deputy – and an Irish privy council, both appointed by the crown. However, this Dublin-based executive government was subordinate to the English crown. There was an Irish parliament, like that of England comprising an upper chamber of spiritual and temporal lords and a lower chamber of elected representatives, which might more closely reflect the population of Ireland, but its membership could be manipulated by the English crown and its powers were limited. Under

Tudor statutes, the prior approval of the English crown was required before a parliament could be summoned and before any legislation could be introduced into it. These statutes ensured that both the Irish parliament and the Dublin-based executive would remain subservient to, and tightly controlled by, the English crown. Neither on paper nor in practice were they subordinate to the English parliament. Although substantial numbers of Scots were resident in Ireland, they were largely excluded from the English-controlled government of Ireland, and the Scottish government had no direct involvement in the Irish legislature or executive.

Like both Wales and Ireland, medieval Scotland had been imperfectly united and was prone to internal division and strife. By the late sixteenth century, however, the Scottish crown had succeeded in extending its power throughout much of the kingdom, curbing the great family and clan feuds and imposing a greater degree of royal control over the borderlands of the south and the highlands of the north. However, Scotland remained markedly less unified than England, for the clans retained a strong influence in the highlands and islands, the nation was divided linguistically between the mainly English-speaking lowlands and the still largely gaelic highlands, and effective royal control over parts of the highlands and western isles, especially those formerly covered by the 'Lordship of the Isles' and extending across the North Channel to embrace the mainland of north-east Ireland, was at best diluted. Compared to that of England, central government was small, informal and less developed. The king ruled with the assistance of a privy council and of occasional, infrequent parliaments. The latter, which met to adjudicate disputes, make new laws and grant new taxes, comprised members of the peerage and the landed class, representatives of the burghs, officers of state and some churchmen, sitting together in a single chamber. At the beginning of each parliament a small committee, the lords of the articles, would be elected, with powers to sift through proposed legislation and to put together a package of approved bills which would then be placed before the parliament as a single parcel and voted for en bloc. Royal control over the summoning and dissolution of parliaments, and royal influence over the lords of the articles, together ensured that the Scottish parliament was generally subservient to the crown.

Like kings of England, the early modern Scottish crown relied heavily upon the goodwill and co-operation of the landowners. The crown lacked a large, standing army and the financial resources to create and maintain one, and so possessed limited coercive powers of its own. The Scottish and English crowns alike looked to win respect and co-operation in part by emphasising the sacred and divine nature of kingship and in part by stressing that a strong monarchy would give stability to the social hierarchy and serve as a bulwark against chaos. However, the early modern Scottish crown was weaker than the English crown. Unlike England, on several occasions during the sixteenth century Scotland had suffered severe internal unrest and disorder, born of monarchical minority or inadequacy. Moreover, even in the more ordered and stable seventeenth century, Scottish royal power in the highlands and islands was far weaker than the power of the English monarch in the provinces. And Scottish kings ruled a thinly populated nation – probably numbering well under a million in the early seventeenth century – with an economy far smaller and less developed than that of England and with a royal income dwarfed by that of the English crown.

These stark contrasts between England and Scotland were always important, but they were driven home from 1603 when the reigning king of Scotland succeeded to the throne of England on the death of the childless Elizabeth I. Thereafter, the two kingdoms shared a common monarch, but moves towards fuller political union were initially unwelcome in both Scotland and England and were firmly rebuffed. During most of the seventeenth century it was a regal union, but nothing more. Thus Scotland retained its own privy council, parliament and judicial system, quite separate from, and theoretically independent of, the English executive, legislature and judiciary. However, the two governments were far from equal, for after 1603 the Scottish king became an absentee, as James hurried south to claim his inheritance; he returned only once thereafter, in 1617. After his death in 1625 the Scots were effectively ruled by an Englishman, for Charles I, although born in Dunfermline, had been brought up in England and had few direct contacts with Scotland. As king, he visited Scotland just twice, in 1633 to be crowned and in 1641 to make peace. Although royal government continued to act through the Scottish privy council, the king himself was governing Scotland from London and, if he chose to seek and to follow it, upon the advice of London-based politicians. Many Scots were acutely aware that the interests of their monarch's far more powerful English kingdom might take precedence over their own.

The reign of James VI and I and its legacy

From 1603 England, Wales, Ireland and Scotland shared a single ruler, but the relationships between them remained complex. Politically Wales had been absorbed by England, Ireland was a dependency of England and a

11

conquered land, and Scotland was an independent nation under a shared monarch. Apart from the monarch himself and his royal court, now based in southern England, there was no central institution empowered to control the three kingdoms. Each had its own privy council and parliament, those of Scotland and Ireland answerable to the monarch, who might seek the advice of his English privy council on Scottish and Irish matters, but not to the English legislature. The Scots and Irish feared being swallowed up by England as Wales had been, and they strongly opposed that form of union and vigorously defended their rights. In any case, after moves towards full Anglo-Scottish union had collapsed during the opening years of James's reign, he and his son moved slowly. The focus of royal policy seemed to switch to one of gradual convergence or congruity, of smoothing away some of the grossest inconsistencies between the three kingdoms.

Both James I and Charles I wished to consolidate and, where possible, extend their powers within each of their three kingdoms, and both, struggling with financial systems which were under strain, sought in a variety of ways to boost royal income. In each kingdom new taxes required the approval of a representative assembly, and in each both James and Charles did, from time to time, summon parliaments for this purpose. More controversially, the crown might revive and exploit more fully existing sources of income, many of them springing from elements of the medieval feudal system. Although this might boost royal income, it also risked provoking disharmony and discontent, for in each kingdom there was an expectation that monarchs should seek wider, generally parliamentary, consent in finding additional sources of income. Again, James and Charles did pursue this line in their kingdoms and both encountered some opposition. Even more dangerously, the crown might challenge existing landowners to demonstrate clear title to their estates and, where they proved unable to do so, might either impose a fine for confirming the title or seize part or all of the estate. In the light of the great upheavals which had occurred in Scotland and Ireland during the sixteenth century, the Stuart crown might find it more fruitful to challenge landowners there than in England and Wales, with their more stable recent history. Although this might improve royal finances and also underline royal authority, if carried too far it might also undermine the social order, so threatening social chaos, or alienate the entire landowning class, so provoking non-co-operation or outright rebellion. After 1603 this policy was pursued by James I in Ireland at least, and after 1625 by Charles I in both Ireland and Scotland.

Both James I and his son also had to wrestle with the complexities of

12

religion and the church in the three kingdoms. England and Wales possessed a single state church, the Church of England, to which everybody had to belong and in which everybody had to worship. The church which had emerged from the Reformation was a sometimes ambiguous amalgam of Catholic and Protestant (especially Calvinist) elements, episcopalian in structure – administered by bishops and archbishops appointed by the crown – and closely tied to the state. By 1603 the great majority of the population were willing members of this church, though there remained a tiny minority of Roman Catholics, outside the law and intermittently persecuted, and a much larger body of Protestants who, although members of the Church of England, felt that the Reformation had not gone far enough. They acted as a sort of pressure group from within, urging further action to purge remaining 'papist' elements from the church and to move it in a 'low' direction.

The official Irish church, the Church of Ireland, was also a Protestant episcopalian church. But only a minority of the population, chiefly the new English descendants of post-Reformation English and Welsh settlers, belonged to this church. In addition, the new wave of early seventeenth-century colonists from lowland Scotland brought with them their own Scottish presbyterian faith. In areas where they dominated, especially Ulster, the Church of Ireland proved flexible enough to accommodate them – both, after all, drew upon Calvinism. However, the great majority of the population in Ireland, including the native Irish and the old English, were Roman Catholics, who had no place in the Church of Ireland and whose religious needs were served by a variety of individual priests and Catholic orders. On paper, Catholicism was not tolerated and Catholic worship was illegal, but in practice the recusancy laws were rarely applied and, so long as they were orderly and politically loyal, the English crown did not persecute Catholics. In reality the crown had little option but to allow *de facto* religious toleration in Ireland, for it did not have the resources to impose Protestantism on an unwilling Irish population.

Scotland was also divided, with a strong legacy of Catholicism among many of the clans of the highlands and islands, but with a reformed Protestant church dominating the lowlands and supported by the crown. The Scottish church was Calvinist in theology and presbyterian in organisation, its structure based upon lay elders and pastors. Although there were some Protestant bishops in Scotland, in the latter half of the sixteenth century they possessed little power and had no real control over the presbyterian church.

As ruler of the three kingdoms James I found himself in a complex

13

religious position. The Church of England was closely tied to the state, for in the course of the sixteenth-century English Reformation the king became supreme head of the church. He also exercised controlling power over the Church of Ireland. The Scottish Reformation had caused a larger degree of separation between church and state and, in consequence, the king was not head of a state church there and would have to fight to impose political control over the presbyterians. There were also religious differences within James's three kingdoms – deeper in Scotland and Ireland than in England and Wales – and between them. The majority of the population in each kingdom supported a form of religion different from the majority religion of the other two. In each kingdom there existed a minority who preferred the religion of another of the three kingdoms. Royal attempts to alter religion within each kingdom or to impose religious unity between them might provoke a religious conflagration.

Given the power of the crown, much would depend upon the character and personality of the monarch in the implementation of religious and other policies for the three kingdoms. Where once historians viewed James I as weak and woefully inadequate, particularly as king of England, over the last generation his reputation as ruler of England from 1603 to 1625 has been revised and he is now generally viewed – by Christopher Durston, S.J. Houston, Barry Coward and others – as a moderate, wise and broadly successful monarch. As interpretations of the causes of the English civil war have changed to emphasise short-term factors, so James's reign is no longer viewed as a staging post on the road to civil war. In 1603 James inherited a number of problems in England, especially an outdated and barely adequate system of state finance and a state church which might be torn asunder by those pressing for further reformation. James did not resolve these fundamental problems, but by tact and flexibility, by seeking short-term solutions and by letting sleeping dogs lie, he provided England with a period of peace and stability. Although probably born of a hatred of war rather than of a deeper awareness of the fiscal and administrative implications, his refusal to commit England to the continental Thirty Years War, even when his parliaments and people were urging him to do so, spared England the enormous and potentially crippling burdens of conflict. His own bearing, his boisterous court and his preference for male favourites were not always edifying, and his personal extravagance undoubtedly worsened a weak financial position and helped to wreck attempts to pull royal finances into the black. On the other hand, his flexible and balanced approach ensured that few would be completely alienated by his regime and implacably oppose it, and that major dislocation would be avoided. This is seen most clearly in James's religious policy, which maintained a balance between those who favoured low church reform and those who opposed it and thus ensured that the Church of England remained a broad state church in which all English and Welsh Protestants could find a place. If James occasionally angered and argued with his parliaments, he generally maintained a good working relationship with the legislature and displayed a willingness to explain his policies. If he occasionally made lofty claims to a much expanded royal prerogative, in practice he played by the established rules and was anxious to act, and to be seen to act, in a just and legal manner. The landowning elite, like some members of the Church of England, might occasionally have been disappointed by James's words or deeds, but they had no cause to feel threatened by him and to withdraw their support.

This cannot be said for all James's Irish subjects. In religious affairs he pursued the same cautious, moderate approach which he displayed in England. As in England, he sought to improve the quality of the Protestant church, encouraging improved training and material support for the clergy and better maintenance of church buildings. With his approval, the Church of Ireland adopted a new set of canons in 1615, strongly Calvinist in tone. On the other hand, despite the laws against Catholicism and occasional royal proclamations against Catholics, in practice James continued the policy of toleration towards the majority Irish faith. Indeed, on several occasions he curbed the over-zealous activities of his Dublin government, preventing strict enforcement of the laws and blocking persecution of the Catholics. But, at the same time, James's approach towards Irish land and colonisation undermined the position of the Irish Catholic population. In the wake of the Elizabethan conquest of Ulster, completed in 1603, and of the flight four years later of the two leading native Irish earls who held land in Ulster, James actively encouraged a programme of renewed Protestant colonisation of that province. Although the colonisation programme did not proceed as quickly as James hoped, and the displacement of the native Irish was not as extensive as he envisaged, he set in train an enormous and far-reaching plantation of Ulster which, by 1640, had seen perhaps 10,000 English and 40–50,000 Scots, the majority of them lowland presbyterians, settling there.

From 1615 James also began to challenge rights to landownership elsewhere in Ireland, resurrecting old claims, some dating back centuries, to royal possession of estates. The aim was not total dispossession, for the challenge usually resulted in the existing landholder being confirmed in

15

possession of much of his estate, although part was often ceded to the crown and thus made available for new English or Scottish plantation. As in Ulster, native Irish landowners seem to have been more deeply affected than the old English, but both groups were apprehensive. Royal policy appeared to be undermining the position of Catholic native Irish and old English alike, if only by ensuring an increase in the number of Protestant Scottish and English settlers in Ireland. Largely excluded from the executive government in Dublin, the Catholics also saw their position within the Irish parliament under threat. In the parliament of 1613 the government deliberately enfranchised Protestant-dominated towns, including the new Scottish settlements in Ulster, to overturn a Catholic majority in the House of Commons. Although protests to the king brought concessions, and the parliament did not proceed with anti-Catholic legislation, apprehensions had been reinforced.

As James VI, James had ruled Scotland in name from 1567 and in practice from the mid-1580s. By 1603, when he left for England, he had successfully extended his authority there, pacifying much of the factionalism of the Scottish aristocracy and thwarting any moves to reassert or extend the Catholic faith. He had also set in train a policy of asserting a degree of royal control over the Scottish presbyterian church. Again, that policy continued after 1603, as James sought not only to extend his power but also to bring the Scottish church closer to an English church which he had found very attractive. In 1606 the Scottish parliament recognised James as supreme governor of the presbyterian church and over the following decade the king moved to cement his royal supremacy. James reinvigorated and empowered the Scottish episcopacy, for the Scottish bishops, like the English, could serve as agents of royal supervision. In the closing years of the reign, James's focus shifted to liturgical matters. At the general assembly – the governing body – of the Scottish church held in Perth in 1618, James forced through five articles introducing new elements into church services, including kneeling at communion and observance of holy days. These changes, which would bring the Scottish church closer to the Church of England, were unpopular, arousing fears of moves towards both Catholicism and religious conformity with the Church of England, which most Scottish Protestants viewed as far less reformed and pure than their own. Although James succeeded in pushing bills through the Scottish parliament of 1621 to give the five articles of Perth statutory authority, they were not strictly enforced and the degree of political and religious hostility encountered in promoting them persuaded him to attempt no further religious reforms during the remainder of his reign.

In 1625, therefore, Charles I inherited three kingdoms which remained divided in religion and in which royal income remained barely adequate to cover peacetime expenses. Moreover, his father's policies had created in Scotland religious apprehension and in Ireland a sense of tenurial insecurity which had strong religious undercurrents. However, he also inherited three kingdoms which were at peace and which had enjoyed a generation of peace, a welcome change for both Scotland and Ireland. With the benefit of hindsight, 1625 appears a turning point in the history of early Stuart government, when James I's caution in handling the three kingdoms gave way to his son's clumsy and provocative approach which, by 1642, had contributed to a collapse in royal power in all three.

3
From peace to war in three kingdoms, 1637–42

Introduction: the kingship of Charles I

In seeking to explain why all three kingdoms dissolved into rebellion and war between 1637 and 1642, it is tempting to focus upon the personality and policies of Charles I. This would be to ignore longer-term institutional problems within and between the three kingdoms which were not of Charles's making and which he inherited in 1625. However, there is broad consensus among historians that Charles's character and his view of kingship created difficulties and that the king must bear a large personal responsibility for provoking the crises which overwhelmed him. Charles was a cold, formal figure who rarely sought to explain himself or to win affection. Instead, he emphasised the majesty of the crown and required unquestioning obedience. Although capable of seeking advice, he often failed to understand viewpoints different from his own and instead equated them with disloyalty. A hard-working monarch of strong convictions, Charles pressed ahead with his policies to extend royal power and to reform the church in an inflexible and unyielding way. Possessing none of his father's willingness to compromise and conciliate, he proceeded even when a policy was arousing great opposition or was proving unworkable, believing that a mixture of divine support, the aura of monarchy, physical force and duplicity could secure adherence. By the early 1640s Charles's inept approach had created a breakdown of trust in each of his kingdoms, which in turn contributed to the outbreak of armed resistance in all three.

Scotland

Scotland was the first of Charles I's three kingdoms to rise against the king. Charles, an absentee king, initiated during the opening decade of his reign policies designed, in his eyes, to make Scottish government more efficient. The structure of the central executive and judiciary was over-hauled, with the deliberate promotion of churchmen, attempts were made to extend royal control over justice and administration in the provinces, and direct and indirect taxes were increased to boost royal income. At the start of his reign Charles launched a policy of revocation, an established procedure whereby a new king of Scotland, upon reaching the age of twenty-five, could recover royal lands lost during his minority. But Charles had not really endured a minority, for he was twenty-five in November 1625, barely eight months after succeeding to the throne. Moreover, Charles indicated that this revocation would be much broader than usual, exploring landownership since 1540 and including former church lands secularised since the Scottish Reformation of the mid-sixteenth century. Although Charles subsequently claimed that his intention had merely been to regularise existing land tenure and to provide better financial support for the Scottish church, revocation seemed to threaten large-scale confiscation. Widespread non-co-operation stifled Charles's scheme, but the whole issue had both aroused the antagonism of the landed elite and shown them that they could successfully oppose royal policy through direct action. On the other hand, they came to see that peaceful opposi-tion to the king was dangerous. In 1635 one of their number, Lord Balmerino, was sentenced to death (though subsequently pardoned) for knowing of, but not revealing to the king, the existence of one of several documents cataloguing the undercurrent of discontent with royal policies.

From the mid-1630s Charles intensified his drive for religious reform in Scotland in order to purge what he viewed as religious impurities, to extend royal control over the church, to reduce the differences between the Scottish and English churches and to bring the former closer to the latter. But he hugely underestimated the power of the Scottish opposi-tion and overestimated his capacity to retain or regain control. Through revocation, he had tried to give the church a more secure financial base. By promoting bishops to secular office, he had given them greater powers. Now Charles moved on to reform the liturgy of the Scottish presbyterian church. In 1636 he imposed a new book of canons (church laws), based upon the English canons of 1604 and embodying the five articles of Perth, which he ordered strictly enforced. By stressing the use of prescribed prayers and ordering that no minister was to preach

19

outside his parish unless licensed by his bishop, the canons permitted tighter royal control over preaching. In 1637, following lengthy preparations, involving selected Scottish bishops as well as the Archbishop of Canterbury, but without wider Scottish consultation, Charles ordered the adoption of a new prayer book. Based on the English prayer book but in some areas reflecting the different Scottish context, the new prayer book reinforced the move from a preaching ministry to more elaborate and rigid ceremonial forms. It aroused strong opposition in Scotland, both for what it said and for what it represented – English control, creeping episcopalianism and an authoritarian crown careless of Scottish feelings. From the outset, then, there was a British dimension to the crisis, for the Scots were responding to the actions of an English-based crown and English-style developments in religion.

The attempt to impose the new prayer book in July 1637 provoked violent resistance and mass petitions aimed also at the new canons and the role and power of bishops. The Scottish privy council was weak and hesitant and royal authority crumbled. When, in February 1638, Charles uncompromisingly insisted that the prayer book be accepted and that continuing resistance would be viewed as treason, the opposition in Scotland drew up a National Covenant. It bound the signatories to support each other and God in defence of the true religion and against religious innovations. Cautious in tone, the religious innovations were neither specified nor explicitly condemned as unlawful and the document made no reference to bishops. Instead, it stressed loyalty and respect to the king, and looked for justification to earlier oaths and statutes against religious innovations. First signed in Edinburgh on 28 February, the National Covenant received mass support in the lowlands and patchier support in the highlands. The Scots probably believed that this written show of strength would make Charles back down.

In the face of such opposition, from spring 1638 Charles began seeking a military solution by using English and Irish resources to impose his religious policy in Scotland. But he also saw the need for religious concessions to win time while he prepared for a military campaign. Acting through the Marquis of Hamilton, a leading Scottish peer, during 1638 Charles offered to revoke the prayer book and the canons, abandon the five articles of Perth, and reduce the power of bishops. A year before this might have resolved the situation, but by autumn 1638 opposition in Scotland had gained such momentum and Charles's repeated threats had aroused such suspicions that the covenanters were not won over. Accordingly, the general assembly of the church which met at Glasgow in November proceeded to vote through not only all Charles's promised concessions but also the complete abolition of episcopacy. It continued to meet after the king ordered it dissolved, and claimed that henceforth general assemblies should meet annually. Together with the changes to the liturgy and organisation of the church, this amounted to a rejection of royal control over the Scottish church, not merely the thwarting of royal plans for reform. This confirmed to Charles that only military intervention could retrieve his position in Scotland.

The king's decision to seek a military solution and to commit two of his kingdoms to war against the third brought the British nature of the crisis into sharp focus. During the winter of 1638–9 the king made detailed preparations for a military assault upon the Scots in 1639, employing English and Irish military resources. In response, the Scots raised an army and also sought help not only from their compatriots and co-religionists in Ulster but also from the English. Scottish propaganda, seeking to woo Englishmen who had misgivings about the king's policies in England, stressed that the Scots intended no harm to England, respected the king and the regal union, and were fighting merely to protect themselves against religious innovation and a popish plot. By 1639, and perhaps from 1637–8, clandestine links had been established between the covenanters and some leading English opponents of royal policies.

The covenanters were now effectively in control of Scottish central government and of local government in the lowlands and much of the highlands – episcopalian enclaves in Aberdeen and the north-east were guarded or overawed – and they successfully gathered the resources needed to defend the country. Charles planned a quadruple attack. In Ireland, Lord Deputy Sir Thomas Wentworth was to raise an army of 10,000 men, which was to attack south-west Scotland. To the dismay of some of his own supporters the king also commissioned the Earl of Antrim, the leading Catholic Scot in north-east Ireland, to raise a separate army which was to attack the west coast of Scotland, an area in which Antrim had both extensive family connections and expansive territorial ambitions. The Marquis of Hamilton was to lead an amphibious force of 5,000 men to assault the east coast and to serve as a naval blockade. Finally, the king was to raise an army of 20,000 Englishmen and lead it across the border. In fact, Charles seems to have believed that little or no fighting would be necessary as Scottish resistance would melt away when faced by their king in arms.

The reality was very different. Very unusually, the king did not seek English parliamentary support for the conflict, but instead went to war

21

financed by loans and non-parliamentary exactions, the income from which dwindled during 1639. Although there was little enthusiasm for the war, Charles encountered no open English resistance to it and by May had gathered around Berwick an army of 15,000 men. On 4 June 4,000 men marched to Kelso, but turned tail when faced with the Scottish covenanter army under General Alexander Leslie. Far from melting away, the Scottish army seemed ready to fight, and Leslie menacingly drew up his troops just across the Tweed from the English camp. With Irish assistance failing to materialise and Hamilton's fleet achieving little, Charles felt compelled to open negotiations. The Scots were reluctant to attack the king or invade England for fear of alienating English sympathies and uniting England behind Charles. Some of the English aristocracy probably also wanted peace, viewing war with Scotland as not in the interests of England. Indeed, for those who opposed Charles's policies in England, a clear royal victory would have been unhelpful. Accordingly, the First Bishops' or Scots' War of 1639 was brought to a swift end by the pacification or truce of Berwick in June 1639. Many of its terms were vague and ambiguous, both sides clearly viewing it as merely a temporary cessation of arms.

As part of the truce, a general assembly and parliament met in the autumn. Dominated by covenanters, they pushed ahead with aggressively anti-royal policies, repeating and re-enacting most of the religious reforms of the 1638 Glasgow assembly, but also more explicitly condemning episcopacy as contrary to God's will. This threatened the episcopalian churches of England and Ireland as well as royal hopes to retain Scottish bishops. Before obeying the king's order to prorogue in November 1639, parliament established a committee to represent it when it was not sitting. Covenanter control was made clear when parliament reassembled in summer 1640, in defiance of the king, and swiftly passed a legislative programme which amounted to a constitutional revolution. Ecclesiastical representation in parliament and the right of officers of state to sit were abolished, as was the vetting of draft legislation and other business at the start of the session. A Triennial Act was passed, laying down that a parliament was to meet at least once every three years, even if there had been no royal summons. A new executive committee was established to oversee government after parliament rose. New taxes were voted to support the imminent renewal of hostilities and the executive committee was given additional powers to direct the war effort. Although the legislation was forwarded to the king, his consent was not sought. Instead, it was implied that it had full statutory power whether or not the king expressed an opinion.

Long before this time, Charles had decided to resume war against Scotland, his determination apparently unaffected by the failure of the English parliament which he had called in spring 1640 to support the conflict. English mobilisation was slow and met clear resistance. As a result, the two supporting arms of a planned three-pronged attack, an assault upon south-west Scotland by an army which Wentworth was raising in Ireland and an English amphibious attack upon the east coast, were aborted. Seizing the initiative, on 20 August the Scottish covenanter army crossed the border, by-passed Berwick and made for Newcastle. On 28 August a Scottish army of over 15,000 men threw back an English force of around 5,000 which tried to hold the Tyne at Newburn, and proceeded to occupy Newcastle and most of northern England. Charles had lost the Second Bishops' or Scots' War in a single engagement.

The king had tried to use two of his kingdoms to crush the third, but had failed disastrously. The Scots now wanted a durable religious and political settlement and believed that this could not be achieved by negotiating with the king alone or by seeking a purely separate Scottish treaty. Instead, they now pressed for a truly British settlement, embracing England and Ireland and ratified by the parliaments of England, Scotland and, where appropriate, Ireland too. They had invaded England in pursuit of this broader settlement and their occupation of northern England, the subsequent imposition of a financial levy of £850 per day and their control of the Tyneside coalfields, upon which London relied, were designed to bring it closer by ensuring that Charles I was as powerless in England as he was in Scotland. Defeated in war and financially crippled, Charles was left no option but to summon another English parliament, to keep it in existence and to make a string of concessions to it. After a truce had been concluded at Ripon in October 1640, the Scottish covenanters despatched commissioners to London to negotiate with royal commissioners and the new English parliament the terms of a firm peace treaty which the Scots hoped would encompass the three kingdoms.

The opponents of Charles I in the English parliament, aware that their strength was dependent upon the Scots, worked closely with them and supported several Scottish demands, including the punishment of Charles's leading ministers, especially Archbishop William Laud and Wentworth, now Earl of Strafford. Parliament and the king swiftly accepted many of the Scottish proposals for a final peace treaty, including confirmation of the Scottish parliament's 1640 legislation. However, Scottish demands for a broader, British dimension to the treaty met with apathy or opposition from both the king and the English parliament. Under article eight of the proposed treaty of London, the Scots pressed for a closer, more federal-type union between England and Scotland – with the two nations retaining a large measure of internal independence but accepting mechanisms to ensure compatibility and close co-operation. In terms of religion they wanted uniformity, with the English episcopalian church replaced by a presbyterian-type church. They – much like the king – believed that firm, durable peace was impossible so long as the two kingdoms had different churches; but unlike Charles, they believed that uniformity should be based upon the supposedly purer Scottish church. In political terms, the Scots sought close co-operation between the English and Scottish parliaments when sitting, and between bodies of English and Scottish commissioners in the intervals between parliaments, agreement that neither England nor Ireland was to make war against Scotland without the approval of the English parliament, and vice versa, and an Anglo-Scottish military alliance against outside attack. The Scots also sought closer commercial co-operation. The king and the English parliament were firmly opposed to the Scots' proposal for religious union and had little interest in most of their plans for political, military and commercial links. The Scottish proposals, especially for wholesale reform of the Church of England, were going too far, even for many English critics of the king. Thus they threatened to divide the opposition to him and might enable the king to rally support.

Charles I visited Scotland in summer 1641 to ratify the treaty. The Scots had been forced to shelve plans for religious union, but the final treaty included watered-down versions of their proposals for closer Anglo-Scottish political, military and commercial co-operation, though they were thereafter largely ignored by both the king and the English parliament. The treaty did bring peace, and during August 1641 the Scots withdrew from England and disbanded much of their army. It also confirmed the constitutional revolution of 1640. Indeed, the king was forced to go further, accepting that Scottish legislation did not require the royal assent, and that Scottish political and judicial officers could henceforth be appointed only with the approval of the Scottish parliament. The king, left with very little power in Scotland, had probably seen the need to make massive concessions to the Scots to get them out of English political and military affairs and leave him free to focus on his English troubles. But in failing so conspicuously, and in conceding so much, he probably further destabilised both England and Ireland.

The Scottish covenanters had achieved all they wanted in internal religion and politics, and had done so with little bloodshed and a remarkable degree of unity. Some fracture lines had become apparent, including pockets of potentially pro-royalist, pro-episcopalian sentiment in the north-east, growing personal disaffection between some prominent covenanters, especially the powerful Earls of Argyll and Montrose, and by 1640–1 broader but muted misgivings that the movement was going too far in undermining the power and status of the Scottish crown and in attempting to interfere in English affairs. However, down to 1642 none of these seriously divided the covenanter movement, and the country had been ostensibly united in successful opposition to royal policies for Scotland. As yet, the king had been unable to acquire a significant party within Scotland, and a botched plot – 'the Incident' – to kidnap or assassinate some of the covenanter leaders during the royal visit of 1641, which may or may not have had the knowledge or approval of the king, did little to win him friends on either side of the border. But covenanter hopes of achieving a broader British settlement by creating closer Anglo-Scottish political and religious links and, through them, some control over Irish affairs, had largely been thwarted. In their eyes, the treaty of London was imperfect. The Scots, the first of Charles's peoples to rise in arms against him and to have British resources deployed against them, triggered a British crisis and sought a British settlement.

Ireland

In the opening years of his reign Charles was under particular pressure, for he was at war with both France and Spain. In consequence he offered a number of concessions to the Irish in order to win their financial support. Referred to as 'matters of grace and bounty' or 'the graces', they formed a broad reform programme, parts of which would benefit all sections of the population in Ireland. However, many were of particular benefit to the Catholics, for they would curb anti-Catholic measures and allow them greater rights. Above all, the crown offered to renounce any claims to land titles of more than sixty years' standing, which would give security to most landowners and severely curtail both Catholic dispossession and Protestant colonisation. Although not extending full religious or political rights, the graces would improve the position of Catholics and were welcomed by the native Irish and the old English. Conversely, many new English were dismayed, for royal concessions to Catholics seemed to threaten their own religious and political dominance. Despite royal assurances, most graces were not confirmed in law by the Irish parliament and, as they remained reliant upon the king's goodwill, could easily be reversed. Their confirmation in statutory form became a major Catholic objective.

By the time Thomas Wentworth was appointed as lord deputy of Ireland at the end of 1631, peace had been concluded with Spain and France, and the king had less cause to treat Ireland gently. Wentworth did not cross to Dublin until summer 1633. He left for the last time in spring 1640 and his political control there effectively ended soon after. His seven-year regime saw the intensification of several existing royal policies, together with the imposition of new religious policies favoured by Charles I. Wentworth placed royal finances in Ireland upon a firmer footing, and continued the policy of plantation, focusing on the north-western province of Connacht and dispossessing many – mainly old English – landowners there, though he found it difficult to attract English settlers and was determined to prevent further Scottish plantation. In religion, Wentworth continued to allow the Catholic majority to practise their faith undisturbed. At the same time, he attempted to increase the lands and income of the Protestant Church of Ireland by seeking to recover former church property secularised since the Reformation. This appeared to threaten the holdings of many of the recent new English settlers as well as some old English who, although Catholics, had bene-fited from the secularisation of former church lands. Wentworth also imposed Charles's favoured high church policies on the Church of Ireland, setting up an Irish court of high commission to impose conformity.

By the late 1630s Wentworth had alienated all the major groups in Ireland. The native Irish and the old English were dismayed by his continuing refusal to allow statutory confirmation of most graces. Both groups, but particularly the old English, were threatened by the policy of land dispossession. The new English and the Scottish presbyterians were alienated by Wentworth's religious policy; his attempts to recover former church land also threatened some old English. The Scots were aware of his dislike of them and they, like some new English, were enraged when he interfered in some Ulster plantations. Because of Wentworth's author-itarian manner, the new English found that they now wielded far less political influence in Dublin. Wentworth made no serious effort to culti-vate an Irish power-base, relying instead upon the authority of the English crown to sustain his regime. When the crown's power was frag-mented by the Scots in 1639–40, Wentworth's anglicising regime, and with it royal control over Ireland, quickly collapsed.

From the outset, Ireland had been drawn into the unfolding Scottish crisis of the late 1630s. The large Scottish presbyterian community in

Ulster was seen by Wentworth as a danger, threatening either to provide military support for the Scots on the British mainland or to rise up in Ireland against Charles I's Irish regime. Accordingly, from the winter of 1638–9 Wentworth took care to neutralise the presbyterian Scots of Ulster by stationing much of the existing, modest army at his disposal there and imposing upon the Scots an oath disavowing the Scottish covenant and pledging loyalty to Charles I. Many Ulster Scots returned to Scotland in the face of this pressure. At the same time, Ireland was also seen as a potential source of pro-royalist troops who could be deployed by Charles against the Scots. In 1638–9 plans were laid for Wentworth to raise an Irish army and for the Earl of Antrim to raise a separate force among the mainly Catholic enclave of the north-east. In reality, the First Bishops' War was over so quickly that there was no direct Irish military involvement in 1639, though the king's projected use of Irish forces, especially those to be raised by Antrim, probably strengthened the covenanter cause and persuaded some uncommitted Scots, including the Earl of Argyll, to join the covenanters. In 1639–40, however, Wentworth did succeed in raising an army of around 9,000 men, officered by Protestants but including Catholics, with the intention of launching it against the Scottish mainland. Again, the war was over before this army could be deployed, but its existence raised alarm in England as well as Scotland.

Wentworth, recently created Earl of Strafford, left Ireland apparently secure for the last time in spring 1640, better to serve his king in England. But even before the Second Bishops' War had been fought and lost, his Irish regime was collapsing in his absence, partly because of the strains imposed by raising and maintaining a large Irish army, partly because by this time many of the new English were no longer supporting royal policies; opposition to royal policies in the brief English parliament of spring 1640 probably emboldened the Irish. All groups in Ireland joyfully joined in the criticism of Strafford which erupted from summer 1640 and which reached full voice in the English parliament summoned by Charles in the autumn, in the wake of his Scottish defeat. The Irish parliament compiled a wide-ranging condemnation of Strafford's policies as governor of Ireland and this 'remonstrance', together with other Irish material, provided many of the charges levelled against Strafford in England in the attempted impeachment and successful attainder of spring 1641. During the winter of 1640–1 there was clear and close co-operation between prominent Irish politicians and some leading opponents of the king in the English parliament. The Irish representatives who carried the remonstrance to the English parliament stayed on in London to liaise and to serve as an Irish lobby there. They ran up against Scottish attempts to encompass Ireland within the treaty of London, including moves to restructure religion in Ireland and proposals that henceforth Ireland was to make war on Scotland only with the approval of the English parliament, a provision the Scots sought in vain to have ratified by the Irish parliament.

Irish politics have an air of drift and uncertainty during 1641, in the wake of the power vacuum created by the removal of Strafford and the Scots' defeat of the king. Charles was focusing more on his Scottish and English problems than on Irish developments. A new lord lieutenant, the Earl of Leicester, was appointed, but was absent in France. With royal control slackened, the initiative passed to the Irish parliament, which worked to promote Irish liberties and to secure limitations over the power exercised by an English-appointed executive. The Irish parliament asserted its right to impeach Irish officials, to draft its own legislation and to pass those bills direct to the king for approval, so removing the involvement of the Irish executive in the process. It also drew up a series of 'queries' concerning alleged abuses of power during the 1630s – the imposition of monopolies, the right of the lord lieutenant or deputy to fine and imprison, and so forth – and sought judicial clarification that these practices were illegal, so guaranteeing fundamental liberties. The old English also sought both a royal pronouncement that no further colonisation of Ireland would take place and statutory confirmation of all the graces, including the confirmation of title to all estates held for sixty years. The new English opposed this. Instead, they sought from the king a reversal of high church reform of the Church of Ireland, an end to enquiries into rights to former church lands and income secularised since the Reformation, and a return of all such lands and income reclaimed by the church over the past few years. The Irish might agree on political and administrative reform designed to safeguard Irish rights, but as soon as matters turned to religion, landholding and plantation, wide divisions opened. The king made some concessions – temporarily halting further plantation and regranting the graces but then changing his mind – but he generally stalled, distracted by other issues and aware that acceptance of some Irish demands would greatly reduce his power and income there.

The summer and autumn of 1641 was a period of fear and suspicion. The army raised by Strafford in 1640 was being disbanded only very slowly. Based mainly in the north, its disbandment had been delayed by the need to find cash to pay it off, by the king's reluctance to see these troops disperse until the Scottish army had departed from northern

England, and by negotiations between the English and Spanish crowns with a view to shipping much of it off to fight for Spain on the continent. The Earl of Antrim claimed, a decade later, that in 1641 he – together with the Earl of Ormond, the man chosen to command the Irish army intended for Scotland – had been engaged by Charles to rally or reassemble the army and to use it to support the king, perhaps against the English parliament. Historians such as Ohlmeyer and Perceval-Maxwell remain deeply divided over what degree of truth, if any, lay behind Antrim's later tales. But early in 1641 Charles was exploring the possibility of keeping the Irish army in being on a long-term basis, and there is no doubt that many in England and Scotland were deeply worried about the continuing presence of this army in Ulster and fearful that it might be used against the mainland. For their part, the Irish Catholics were equally disturbed by the anti-Catholic rhetoric emanating from the victorious Scottish covenanters and the English parliament. The Scots were actively proposing a settlement which would bring a new religious as well as political order throughout the three kingdoms, involving the forcible export of Scottish-style presbyterianism. Having welcomed the novel involvement of the English parliament in Irish politics to help rid them of Strafford, many Irishmen, Protestants as well as Catholics, were also concerned by the English parliament's continuing interest in Irish affairs.

It was the Irish Catholics who had most to fear from the profoundly anti-Catholic English parliament, as well as from the victory in war of the equally anti-Catholic Scots and the plans which the Scots were now laying for Ireland. But the outcome and aftermath of the Scottish wars also provided them with a model, showing how it was possible for one of Charles I's kingdoms to rise up in defence of its religion and political rights. The prominently anti-Catholic line being taken by some Irish and English privy councillors in 1641 did little to reassure Irish Catholics, and the failure of the English in the summer to deliver draft legislation to enable the Irish parliament to give statutory confirmation to the graces may have strengthened their resolve, but plans for an Irish Catholic rising apparently pre-dated these developments. The harassed native Irish of Ulster took the lead, waiting until the autumn to make their move. By then the Scottish army had been largely disbanded and it would be difficult for Scotland or England swiftly to launch a military campaign in response.

During the night of 22–23 October 1641 the Irish rebellion began. Claiming, almost certainly falsely, to be acting with Charles's approval and producing a forged commission from the king, the rebels avowed loyalty to Charles but asserted that only direct action would save their church and faith against an alleged Anglo-Scottish plot to extirpate Catholicism. Although plans to capture Dublin were thwarted, within weeks most of Ireland was in rebellion, as the movement spread south from Ulster. The Catholic old English initially held back, but increasingly during the winter they threw their weight behind the native Irish rebels, mindful of long-standing resentments against the Irish and English governments as well as the outspoken threats being issued by the horrified new English in Ireland and the parliament in London. By the end of the winter most of Ireland was in rebel hands. The new English retained control of Dublin and a few walled towns and castles, while the Scottish planters were holding out in parts of Ulster. Field engagements had been few. However, large numbers of Protestants, most of them new English, some of them Scottish, had been murdered during the opening months of the rebellion, and many more had suffered dispossession, which often resulted in death through starvation and disease. The precise death-toll is unknown and was certainly much inflated in the horror stories spread in England and Scotland, but it is likely that several thousand Protestants – perhaps over 10,000 – died in Ireland during the winter of 1641–2 as a direct consequence of the rebellion. By summer 1642 the rebels were not only physically in control of most of Ireland but were laying plans to consolidate their position through a new political and religious organisation. But by then the Scots and the English were also mounting a direct military response.

Although it surprised many contemporaries, historians such as Perceval-Maxwell and Brian Mac Cuarta suggest that the Irish rebellion had clear antecedents. It sprang in part from long-standing tensions and discontent within Ireland which, because of the complexities of religion, landownership, political power and constitutional control, closely involved both Scotland and England. It also sprang directly from the Scottish crisis and the wars of 1637–40 and from the consequences of those developments in both Scotland and England, which together supplied both a dire threat and the model for a possible solution. In turn, the Irish rebellion had important implications for the unfolding British crisis. Rumours of Charles's involvement in the rebellion, whether or not they had any foundation in truth, increased suspicions of their king among the English and Scots and confirmed the latter in their belief that a solution which applied to just one of the three kingdoms would never last. The religious nature of the rebellion heightened existing religious tensions and underlined religious differences within and between the three kingdoms. Charles, strongly denying any complicity in the rebellion and declaring his determination to crush it, had to look to parliament to finance the resulting military campaign, but this in turn brought into sharp focus the question of whether he might be trusted with an army. Because both English and Scottish settlers were being slaughtered by the rebels, it also gave both nations a keen and legitimate interest in resolving the Irish situation and ensured that all three of Charles's kingdoms would continue to be drawn into an unfolding political and military crisis. Any hopes which the king had of keeping separate the affairs of each kingdom and, after buying peace in Scotland at such a high price, of restoring his control in his other two kingdoms, were wrecked by the Irish Catholic rebellion.

England and Wales

Most historians agree on the principal factors which caused the Scottish and Irish crises. There is no such broad agreement about the causes of the civil war in England and Wales. The focus of interpretations varies between long-term and short-term causes, between constitutional and political – including religious – problems and social and economic tensions, between developments at the centre and in the provinces, and between internal English and Welsh developments and a wider British perspective. That continuing and unresolved debate must be reflected here.

Many historians have claimed that the civil war had long-term causes, which can be traced back to the early sixteenth century or before. Some see those causes as principally social and economic, with tensions springing from long-term changes in the prestige, power and economic vitality of different groups within the social hierarchy, particularly the 'rise' of the gentry, middle classes or bourgeoisie and/or the 'decline' of the aristocracy, and from a shift from a feudal to a capitalist economy. Many, though not all, who have taken this line – as have R.H. Tawney, Eric Hobsbawm, Christopher Hill and Lawrence Stone – hold left-wing or Marxist political views. Other historians, also arguing for long-term causes of the civil war, have seen them as principally political and constitutional. They view the sixteenth and early seventeenth centuries as a period of increasingly frequent and bitter clashes between parliament, particularly the House of Commons, anxious to defend and promote the rule of law, property rights, individual liberties and its own powers, and an autocratic crown, anxious to maintain and extend its authority. Civil war between king and parliament was the inevitable consequence of this long process of rising tension between them. This interpretation is found in the works of Thomas Lord Macaulay, S.R. Gardiner and other nineteenth-century

31

historians of the 'Whig' school – which viewed English history as the story of the slow but linear evolution of rights and liberties – and in those of C.H. Firth, G.M. Trevelyan and others who continued to write in this mould in the early twentieth century.

These long-term explanations went out of fashion in the latter half of the twentieth century. During the 1970s and 1980s many historians, including Kevin Sharpe, Mark Kishlansky and Geoffrey Elton, questioned the existence in Tudor and early Stuart England of long-standing and deep-seated conflict of sufficient depth and seriousness to precipitate civil war. Collectively labelled 'revisionists', they generally focus on short-term factors and trace the causes of the war back no further than the accession of Charles I in 1625, often no further than the late 1630s. They see the personal and political mistakes of the king and other leading politicians during the 1630s and early 1640s as leading to a breakdown of trust and thus provoking civil war.

In recent years the revisionist line has itself been attacked for taking too narrow an approach and underplaying deeper problems. Many historians, including Ann Hughes, Richard Cust and David Underdown, suggest that the mistakes and deficiencies of Charles I and contemporary politicians were underlain by a number of more profound and longer-term factors which contributed to the crisis by creating tension and division both at the centre and in the provinces. The doubling in size of the English population in the century before 1640 probably led to increasing levels of under- and unemployment, poverty, dearth and disorder. Royal finances became increasingly strained because of price inflation, the failure of duties levied by the crown to keep pace with inflation, the monarchs' continuing policy of selling crown land, thereby reducing recurrent income, and the dwindling value of the 'subsidies' or special taxes voted by parliament, caused by increasing underassessment of land and income. Accordingly, the crown looked elsewhere and repeatedly attempted to raise money by non-parliamentary means. Conrad Russell stresses the poverty of the early Stuart crown as a source of tension and distrust. Other historians, such as John Morrill and Mark Stoyle, suggest the centrality of religion, with the desire of some further to reform the Church of England and push it in a 'low' direction clashing with the determination of others to resist such moves, so producing deep-seated religious stresses and fracture lines. The difficulties inherent in ruling a multiple kingdom can be presented as another of these rather deeper and longer-standing problems which faced the early Stuart monarchs.

Largely kept in check, though not resolved, during the reign of James

I, there are indications that many of these tensions worsened during the 1620s, provoked by a slackening of James's grip in old age, the policies and personality of the new king, pressure to enter the continental wars and then the huge strains when England did, disastrously, go to war against France and Spain in the late 1620s, and the rise within the Church of England of a new anti-Calvinist movement, vigorously promoted by Charles I. Many of these issues led to outspoken criticism of the new king in the parliaments called between 1625 and 1629. By the end of the decade, amid an atmosphere of political tension and failure, Charles had determined to make peace abroad and to rule without parliaments.

The Personal Rule of Charles I lasted until 1640. The active leadership of the king and the support provided by the traditional mechanisms of executive and local government ensured that the state continued to function and that everything appeared to run smoothly. Existing revenues were collected more efficiently and Charles revived a number of old feudal levies to boost his income. Until 1638–9 fiscal policy appeared successful, for substantial sums were collected, royal income rose by around 50 per cent and the regime was solvent. Only in 1638–9, with the onset of the Scottish crisis and wars, did payment of the various exactions falter. Although official records show little opposition in principle to royal taxation for much of the 1630s, occasional and unsuccessful legal challenges, and evidence from a range of diaries, journals and other private sources, suggest that there may have been a strong undercurrent of discontent with Charles's financial policies building up throughout the decade, an awareness that, by dispensing with parliaments and parliamentary sources of income, he was not governing as other monarchs had.

Charles personally favoured a high church form of Protestantism, often labelled Arminianism, which emphasised ceremony, ritual and elaborate rites associated with worship, involving an elevated role for the clergy, a greater separation between God and the laity – symbolised by erecting within churches permanent, railed-off altars at the east end – and a willingness to believe that salvation was available to all. In many ways this type of Protestant worship ran directly against the Calvinism which had formed a strand within the reformed Church of England, and which tended to take a simpler, more participatory form, with an emphasis on preaching, biblical interpretation, the sanctity of the sabbath and the predestination of souls to redemption or damnation. Working with Laud, Archbishop of Canterbury from 1633, Charles supported and promoted Arminianism during the Personal Rule, attempting to enforce

33

conformity to new or existing ecclesiastical regulations through the appointment of Arminians, regular episcopal visitations, and the control and discipline of church courts and the king's prerogative courts, especially high commission and star chamber. The degree to which these changes were imposed at parish level depended in part upon the local bishop and the incumbent minister, and it is probable that compromises were made.

Opposition to the religious policies was guarded and muted – hardly surprising in the light of the savage punishment of the few who publicly attacked them – though surviving personal papers may again point to an undercurrent of discontent, as do the ejection of some parish priests from their livings and the emigration of large numbers of laymen and churchmen in search of greater freedom in the New World. In the changed political circumstances of 1640 Charles's religious policies, like his fiscal policies, were bitterly attacked and condemned. Many saw Arminianism as a drift towards the hated Catholicism and believed that Charles had knowingly or unwittingly become involved in a popish plot to overthrow Protestantism. Attempts by some historians, such as Peter White, to argue that Arminianism was not new are unconvincing, and the Arminian attack on many tenets of the existing church seems deeply to have affected many people.

Some historians, notably Kevin Sharpe, see the Personal Rule as a period of harmony and good government, which could have continued almost indefinitely had it not been for outside intervention. However, most historians – including Morrill, Cust, Peter Lake and Kenneth Fincham – see it as a time of gathering tension and discontent and claim that outside intervention merely unleashed a torrent of home-grown animosities. But both groups emphasise the effects of the Scottish crisis within England and agree that the Personal Rule ended when and how it did because of the king's Scottish policies and the reaction they provoked in Scotland. They focused English attention on the king's authoritarian approach and on his desire to impose religious change. His attempt to use military force against Scotland placed great strains upon a vulnerable financial and administrative system while also providing an opportunity more effectively to thwart royal policies. Some within the English political elite had established firm links with the Scottish covenanters by the late 1630s, and many more had come to look on the Scottish cause with a kindly eye, either because they genuinely sympathised with the Scots or because they saw, in successful Scottish resistance, a means by which Charles's power and policies within England might be checked. A difficult and unsuccessful war produced distractions and a slackening of royal control over the country, which in turn led to a sudden fall in the payment and collection of revenue. The king's willingness to employ Irish troops, including Irish Catholics, against the Scots aroused apprehension in England and chillingly brought home the possibility that Charles might seek Irish aid to crush opposition in England. Above all, Scottish military success in the Bishops' Wars forced Charles to turn to the English parliament, and Scottish occupation of northern England in 1640 ensured that he would be forced to make concessions to parliament.

Charles had chosen to rule England and Wales during the 1630s without consulting parliament, even going to war against the Scots in 1639 without summoning one. In spring 1640, with a military bill of over £200,000 outstanding and facing renewed war, Charles and his advisors decided to seek parliamentary support. To their horror, the Short Parliament which met on 13 April 1640 proved overwhelmingly hostile to the king's policies. Far from rallying to the king and swiftly granting money to support war, parliament gave vent to years of pent-up grievances, attacking the crown's religious and fiscal policies during the Personal Rule, weaving in assertions of parliamentary rights and allegations of popish plots, and claiming that grievances must be redressed before supply could be granted. Charles quickly lost patience and angrily dissolved the parliament on 5 May, before it had voted any money. It is clear that some MPs and peers were colluding with the Scots and were determined that the king should gain no help from parliament against Scotland. Some saw that a royal military victory would stymie hopes of achieving political reforms in England and were relieved that the parliament failed. However, most MPs were probably motivated by genuine grievances against the king's English regime and a desire that they be settled before the Scottish issue be addressed.

In the wake of the Second Bishops' War, the Scots and many of the king's English advisors pressed him to summon another English parliament. Hamstrung by defeat, Charles had little option and the Long Parliament commenced on 3 November 1640. Hemmed in on all sides, the king was compelled to make major concessions to parliament. He approved both a Triennial Act, laying down that no more than three years could pass between the dissolution of one parliament and the summoning of another, and an Act stating that the present parliament could not be adjourned, prorogued or dissolved without its own consent, thereby surrendering the royal right of dissolution. From the outset, both the Lords and Commons were overwhelmingly critical of the personnel and policies of the Personal Rule, and by August

1641, when parliament went into brief recess, both had been substantially cleared away. Strafford was attainted and executed, Laud was imprisoned and several of Charles's other councillors fled abroad. A series of statutes abolished or drastically downgraded many of the judicial and fiscal planks which had supported the Personal Rule, including the courts of high commission and star chamber, feudal levies, and the collection of customs duties without parliamentary approval. Charles had been stripped of much of his royal power and income, though no clear alternatives had been provided in their place. Religion was more complex and divisive, for although most MPs and peers wished to strip away the Arminian innovations of the last few years, some wanted to go no further than restoring the Church of England as it had been under Elizabeth I and James I, while others wanted to press ahead with more radical reform, perhaps involving the abolition of the episcopal system or the reorganisation of the state church.

Two divergent paths became apparent during the latter half of 1641. On the one hand, Charles might have a means of recovering his position in England by posing as a defender of tradition, social and political order, and the pre-Arminian Church of England against parliamentary innovation. Many feared that continuing parliamentary reform would destabilise the whole status quo and that no further limitations on royal power were necessary or helpful. The involvement of the Scots in English affairs, especially their support for wholesale religious reform on Scottish lines, perturbed many who had hitherto opposed royal policies and gave credence to Charles's stand as a defender of the English constitution and religion. On the other hand, many members of the political nation felt that they could not trust Charles to abide by the concessions already granted and that they must therefore further limit royal power. They lovingly recounted details of 'the Incident' and of alleged army plots, plans hatched during the late winter and spring of 1641 to use part of the English army, still stationed in northern England, against the English parliament; the king's involvement, if any, is unclear. They conjured up images of a continuing popish plot against English liberties and religion which could only be thwarted by further parliamentary control over the executive. Even after the treaty of London, the Scots continued to lobby for such reforms, and some prominent English opponents of the king, fearful of prosecution for treason for their dealings with the Scots in 1639–40, may have decided to press ahead on the grounds of self-defence. However, it was probably the broader fears of a popish plot and Charles reversing his earlier concessions, together with a desire further to reform the English church, which led to continuing assaults on the royal position.

News of the Irish rebellion reached London at the beginning of November 1641 and had a profound impact upon English politics. Having settled with the Scots, some historians, notably Russell, suggest that Charles might have been able to dispense with the English parliament and return to a period of Personal Rule; that chance now disappeared. The rebellion intensified the atmosphere of crisis and suspicion, with rumours that Charles was involved, even that he had commissioned the rebellion. The popish plot seemed to have begun and there was a belief that further measures were needed to safeguard Protestantism, especially as the king was not above suspicion. Because Scottish settlers in Ulster were under attack, Scotland had a legitimate interest in planning an Anglo-Scottish response and was once more drawn into English politics. Above all, an English army would have to be sent to Ireland and the English parliament would have a major role in financing and supporting the venture. But this brought to the fore the question of military command, for many felt that the king could not be trusted with control over an army and feared that he might employ it closer to home.

During the winter of 1641–2 there was a breakdown of trust within English central government. Opponents of the crown pressed ahead with a series of provocative measures in parliament. A 'Grand Remonstrance' rehearsed a list of alleged royal abuses under Charles I and indicated that further remedies were required. Acts removed bishops from the House of Lords, stripped the king of his power to order the county militias to fight outside their home counties and implied that the raising of the army for Ireland was a matter for parliamentary statute, not the royal prerogative. A Militia Bill, eventually passed without royal assent as the Militia Ordinance, gave parliament, not the king, control over the county militias. In summer 1642 parliament demanded full control over the executive and the armed forces. The king felt threatened but he also saw that a substantial part of the political nation was rallying to his defence – the Grand Remonstrance passed the Commons with a tiny majority. Panicked into an unsuccessful attempt to arrest a handful of his leading political opponents in parliament in early January 1642, Charles quit London soon after and headed north, re-establishing his court at York. The physical separation of the king and his opponents made a civil war possible, though the king's withdrawal from London meant that he began it with a huge disadvantage.

Historians who do not see the civil war as a class conflict, and who

37

focus instead upon political divisions at the centre, have to show how and why differences there spilled over and created the fracture lines within local society necessary for civil war to occur. During 1641 royal censorship over the printed word collapsed, and both king and parliament sought to inform and win over the people via published material. In turn, petitions from towns and counties, addressed to king and parliament during 1641–2, suggest that much of the nation was taking a keen and informed interest in developments at the centre. In 1642 this local opinion, often indicating a strong desire for peace, had to be mobilised to support a war. Some historians, such as Morrill, feel that deep religious differences, between those pressing for further reformation and those wanting to preserve the existing Church of England, were to be found at local level as well as at the centre; they suggest that these religious differences explain both how during 1641–2 the nation as a whole divided and why in summer 1642 large numbers of people were motivated to take up arms. Other historians, such as Underdown, see broader cultural divisions at local level, with religion again prominent but underlain by differences in social structure and economic activity. It is clear that in some areas, such as parts of western England, local society did fracture during 1641–2 and king and parliament found pockets of active, willing support. In other areas, for example Cheshire, such divisions were less distinct and widespread apathy and neutralism seemed stronger.

During the spring and summer of 1642 king and parliament both set about raising armed forces to fight a possible civil war. In seeking to raise troops, parliament looked to the Militia Ordinance for justification, the king to the established medieval practice of issuing Commissions of Array. Both involved empowering groups of supporters in each county to call out the militia and to recruit further troops. Inevitably, in some areas, including Nottinghamshire and Leicestershire, there were verbal and physical clashes between rival groups of commissioners and troops. Equally, attempts by king and parliament to secure some important towns – notably Hull – led to confrontations over the spring and summer. But most historians see the English civil war as beginning on 22 August 1642, when Charles raised his standard at Nottingham.

Although historians remain divided, it is likely that a mixture of long-term tensions and short-term problems, policy decisions and blunders contributed to the outbreak of war. Most historians now pay close attention to the period 1640–2, seeking to assess precisely when and for what reasons the political nation divided into two parties unable or unwilling to resolve their differences within the political arena and prepared to resort to arms. Whereas the political elite had been reasonably united in opposition to royal policies in 1640, by 1642 a substantial part of it had rallied to the king's side, making civil war possible. Some apparently believed that it was now better to support a reformed monarch, who could be trusted to respect the concessions of 1640–1, than to push ahead and risk political, social and religious chaos. Others believed that the king could not be trusted even with the reduced powers of 1641 and that further political and religious reformation was necessary. While the Scottish wars of 1639–40 had brought down the Personal Rule and placed the king within the grip of the English parliament, subsequent Scottish pressure and the Irish rebellion served simultaneously to spur on the king's English opponents, to encourage an English reaction in the king's favour and to undermine opportunities for a peaceful resolution. In 1642, the third of Charles's kingdoms descended into war.

Conclusion: one breakdown or three?

It was no coincidence that, after decades of peace, all three of Charles's kingdoms suffered rebellion or war within three years, 1639–42. Because they were tied together, tensions or violence in one helped destabilise the other two. The Scottish crisis was caused by attempts to impose what were perceived to be English religious forms and political control over Scotland. Charles's attempts to use England and Ireland against the Scots broadened and intensified the British nature of the crisis and ensured that the Scots' victory in war would have repercussions in Ireland and England. Scottish pressure ended the Personal Rule in England and created the conditions in which royal power in England might be curtailed. Scottish moves towards a British settlement exacerbated tensions in Ireland created by English rule, but at the same time Scotland provided the model for a possible Irish solution, thereby helping to trigger the Irish rebellion. That rebellion involved both England and Scotland and pulled them more tightly into a British crisis. In England, it closed off a possible escape route for Charles and encouraged further moves against the king, which in turn helped fuel a reaction in the king's favour. In part, the English civil war was a result of Scottish and Irish developments, just as the Irish rebellion had, in part, been caused by English rule and the Scottish wars. It is unlikely that any of these political crises and military conflicts would have occurred how and when they did if Scotland, Ireland and England had been separate and isolated. It was their interrelationship which dictated the form and timing of the breakdown.

Understandably, historians also search for common factors which might explain why all three kingdoms collapsed into violence within such a brief time-span. That search has produced two principal explanations. First, they were all subjected to the rule of Charles I, a king who was seen to be tactless, unwilling to compromise, dishonest and untrustworthy, and generally inept, and who adopted an innovative and authoritarian approach, careless of the rights, liberties and property of his people. In all three of his kingdoms, many came to believe that their property and liberty were threatened by him. Second, all the kingdoms were divided internally and from one another in religion. Many people, in all three kingdoms, took up arms in defence of their religious beliefs and their church, convinced that they were under threat – in Scotland and England from royal policies, in Ireland from the aspirations of the victorious Scots and the English parliament – and that only naked force would preserve them. Some historians see religion as the only element with sufficient depth and force in the centre and in the localities to drive the peoples of the three kingdoms to war against their neighbours.

On the other hand, it would be wrong to overplay these common British elements. The crises and conflicts in Scotland, Ireland, and England and Wales occurred at different times and took different forms. They occurred in kingdoms whose histories, political organisations, religious systems and cultural, racial and religious compositions were very different from one another. In Scotland, the conflict took the form of a war against royal government. The Scots remained substantially united in a national war against an external force. By 1641 they had secured many of their goals, winning a large degree of political and religious autonomy, though they had failed to achieve a broader, British settlement. In Ireland, bloodshed resulted from the rising of a substantial part of the population, which began long after the Scottish wars were over and several months after the resulting peace treaty had been signed. It was triggered by fears of Scottish and English parliamentary interference, but resulted from long-standing internal divisions as well as resentment at royal policies. Because of the deeply divided nature of Irish society, the conflict settled down into a long, internal war, though one kept simmering by external English and Scottish involvement. The goals of the Irish Catholic rebels, to secure the rights and liberties of the Catholic population and to curtail or perhaps remove Protestant control over Ireland – to achieve an Irish Catholic autonomy mirroring the newly won Scottish presbyterian autonomy – had been brought much closer by 1642 but remained elusive. England was the last of the three kingdoms to descend into war and was the only kingdom in which, as the political crisis unfolded, the king gathered a substantial body of support, ensuring that when violence erupted it did so in the form of a civil war fought by two parties of roughly equal size. The goals of the English parliamentarians were ambiguous, though most probably believed they were fighting to defend their religion and property and to ensure that royal power was tightly controlled. It took years of military and constitutional battles before many parliamentarians believed they were coming close to achieving those goals. The three kingdoms had become bound together in a conflict which would continue for most of the 1640s. The routes by which they had travelled and the causes which had brought them to that point had much in common, but were not identical.

4

The British wars, 1642–7

Introduction: the nature of the three wars

The political and military crises in the three kingdoms in the period down to 1642 thereafter spawned wars within and between them. The course of the war within each kingdom was affected by, and in turn influenced, the wars within its two neighbours. However, the combatants showed varying commitment to the idea of a broader British conflict and a potential British settlement. The Scots displayed the strongest commitment, for they sought directly to shape the outcome of the wars in Ireland and England and Wales in a Scottish mould, and so produce a coherent British settlement. The English and Welsh probably showed the least interest in the wider British aspect, for they were caught up in their own intensive civil war and, although both sides sought Scottish and Irish support to help them win that internal civil war, their focus was upon an English and Welsh, not a British, solution. The Irish stand somewhere between the two, the majority Catholic population well aware of Ireland's vulnerability to English and Scottish intervention, and seeking through external negotiation and very limited military intervention to secure a new Irish order within the broader British context.

Scotland

The covenanters' control of Scotland remained secure for much of the period 1642–7 and both central and local government were in their hands. They chose to commit Scotland to a series of wars during this period. In part, these were defensive wars, fought to protect the Scottish homelands, the political and religious achievements of 1641, and Scottish settlers elsewhere. In part, however, they appear interventionist, fought to enhance Scottish influence in England and Ireland, to export the Scottish religion, and to secure the type of British settlement on Scottish terms unsuccessfully sought in 1641.

The Scots took a keen interest in events in Ireland from the outbreak of the rebellion, their concern intensifying during the winter of 1641–2 as the Irish Catholics gained control. The Scots wished to help Scottish settlers in Ireland, especially Ulster, and feared that Catholic control of Ireland would threaten Scotland, either through invasion of the Scottish mainland or by a rising of Scottish Catholic enclaves in the highlands and islands in support of an Irish-backed religious crusade. Moreover, successful Scottish intervention in Ireland would throw back Catholicism, advance Scottish presbyterianism, give the Scots access to land confiscated from Irish Catholics, thus boosting Scottish colonisation of Ireland, and generally bring closer a British settlement on Scottish terms.

During the closing weeks of 1641 Charles I encouraged the Scots to intervene in Ireland. They, however, were wary, anxious that the English parliament should not only approve Scottish involvement but also agree terms and conditions. There was some delay, both because the English parliament was distracted by differences with the king in England and because some MPs and peers were reluctant to give the Scots too much political influence in Irish affairs. Eventually it was agreed that the Scots should raise, arm and despatch to Ireland an army of 10,000 men, which would be paid by England and given two Ulster towns as secure bases. The first wave of 2,500 Scots crossed to Ireland in April 1642, the remainder later in the year. By the end of 1642 a little over 11,000 Scottish officers and men were in Ulster, under the command of Robert Munro (or Monro).

Munro's Scottish army quickly restored order and Protestant control in much of Ulster, but thereafter lost impetus and support. The English parliament proved a poor pay-master, the army was often undersupplied and, because of a failure to impose a clear hierarchy of command and personal animosities between the various commanders, it did not co-operate with other anti-Catholic forces in Ulster. While appreciating the Scottish military contribution, many Ulster Protestants were suspicious of the redistribution of property or political influence which might follow a crushing Scottish victory. When in 1643 the king made a truce with the Irish Catholics, the Scottish and English parliaments alike agreed to keep Munro's army in Ireland to tie down potentially proroyalist forces there. His army did ensure the survival of Protestant control and Scottish influence over much of Ulster, and in the process brought to that province a much stronger, better organised presbyterian church. But its military impact elsewhere was limited and it steadily lost men through disease and the return of units to Scotland. By June 1646, when defeated by Irish Catholic forces at Benburb, near Armagh, it had shrunk to barely 5,000 men. Many survivors returned to Scotland soon afterwards, though the army was not completely disbanded until 1647–8. Scotland's military involvement in Ireland had brought limited rewards.

During 1643 both sides in the English civil war turned to Scotland in search of support. The covenanters initially sought rather to mediate between king and parliament and in the process to bring about a durable British settlement. The king's refusal to negotiate and his rejection of Scottish mediation served to alienate the covenanters and to make a Scottish alliance with the English parliament more likely. Rumours of the king's dealings with the Irish Catholics, which led to the truce of September 1643, allegations of royalist intrigues to provoke proroyalist risings in Scotland and indications that the king was gaining the upper hand in England and Wales during the summer of 1643 all persuaded the covenanters to make a military alliance with the English parliament, despite the despairing efforts of Hamilton and other proroyalist Scottish peers to keep Scotland neutral. The English parliament probably wanted a simple military alliance, but the Scots sought and in part obtained additional commitments to work for closer Anglo-Scottish political and religious ties. The final deal, the Solemn League and Covenant, was agreed in outline during August 1643 and revised and ratified by both sides during September and October.

The Solemn League and Covenant formalised the Anglo-Scottish military alliance, underlined by agreements that the English parliament would finance a Scottish army fighting in England, provide naval support if the Scottish mainland appeared threatened by invasion from Ireland, give future military support on land if the Scots requested it, and agree a truce or peace with the king only with Scottish consent. But the Scots had to accept a dilution of their aspirations for closer political and religious union. Instead of a commitment to full implementation of the treaty of London, the final document spoke vaguely of preserving peace and co-operation between the two nations. Above all, the religious clause had been watered down, with a commitment to reform the English church along Scottish lines dropped in favour of an agreement to reform it 'according to the word of God'. The English parliament wanted Scottish military support so badly that it preferred ambiguity rather than make its opposition to Scottish aspirations explicit. The Scots were aware of the ambiguities, but they feared the consequences for Scotland of a clear military victory for the king in England and probably hoped that a decisive Scottish contribution to the eventual victory of the English parliament would give them a dominant voice in any subsequent settlement.

In Scotland the Solemn League and Covenant met with wide support and, initially, no armed resistance. During the winter of 1643–4 the Scottish covenanters raised an army of a little over 21,000 men under Alexander Leslie, now Earl of Leven, with David Leslie and William Baillie commanding the horse and foot respectively. It crossed the Tweed on 19 January 1644, secured most of Northumberland and County Durham over the following weeks, and then linked with English parliamentary forces to besiege York during the spring and to defeat the royalist army at Marston Moor in July. Thereafter, however, despite receiving further reinforcements of up to 8,000 men, the Scottish army met with limited success in England and its shortcomings, often exaggerated, attracted much English criticism. From late summer 1644 the Scottish covenanters were distracted by pro-royalist military campaigns at home, and Scottish resources were divided by the need to wage war in both Scotland and England, as well as maintaining the Ulster campaign. Although the Scots decided against withdrawing completely from the English theatre to focus on enemies at home, over one-third of the Scottish army in England was recalled, and those forces that remained preferred to stay north of the Trent rather than campaigning against the still potent royalist threat in the Midlands and southern England, far from the Scottish border.

Early in 1644 the king had authorised Antrim to raise 2,000 men in Ireland to attack western Scotland, and Montrose, by now completely alienated from the covenanter cause and openly pro-royalist, to raise 1,000 men in northern England to attack across the border. Although both Montrose's initial venture and a minor pro-royalist rising in northeastern Scotland quickly collapsed, Antrim's Irish forces, led by Alastair MacDonald (or MacColla), successfully landed in July 1644 in the far west, an area where the MacDonalds had territorial claims against the powerful Campbell family, headed by Argyll, one of the most prominent covenanters. This Irish army was soon joined by Montrose, who gathered further Scottish support, mainly among anti-presbyterian, anti-Campbell, often Catholic clans in the highlands and islands. Montrose welded these men into an effective army which launched a successful twelve-month campaign through and around the fringes of the highlands. Between September 1644 and September 1645 Montrose crushed a succession of larger covenanter armies, plundering town and countryside as he went. Although the battles were generally small, involving fewer than 4,000 men on each side, by August 1645 Montrose had defeated most of the covenanter forces in Scotland and entered Glasgow unopposed.

By then, however, it was clear that, unaided, the king would soon lose the war in England. But when, in order to support royalism south of the border, Montrose attempted to leave the highland zone and march south, many of his men deserted him. His depleted forces were surprised and destroyed at Philiphaugh, near Selkirk, on 13 September by part of the covenanter army in England recalled to deal with the threat. Montrose's campaign had temporarily undermined covenanter control of Scotland and had severely weakened Scottish military involvement in Ireland and England, as men were recalled to counter the threat at home. But his reliance upon Irish Catholic forces and the brutality of his campaign had tainted his cause in the eyes of many Scots, he was on bad terms with several potentially pro-royalist fellow-peers and he had failed to win support in the lowlands. Montrose stretched but did not break covenanter resources, undermined but did not end covenanter political control.

By the time the threat posed by Montrose was at an end, the English civil war too was in its final stages. At the beginning of 1644 the Scots had been accorded a political voice by the English parliament by gaining several seats within the principal English executive committee, renamed the committee of both kingdoms. However, they were heavily outnumbered and in practice had been able to exert very little political influence in England during 1644–5. The English parliament showed no inclination to move towards the closer Anglo-Scottish political union which the Scots sought. The king was equally dismissive of Scottish-backed proposals for closer Anglo-Scottish co-operation put to his representatives at Uxbridge in the opening weeks of 1645, as part of abortive peace negotiations. In military terms, after Marston Moor the Scottish contribution to the civil war in England and Wales had been limited and had been deliberately downplayed in the English parliament and press. The Scottish army in England was steadily shrinking and most of it remained in the north, where the war was all but over; only with great reluctance did part of the Scottish army campaign in the West Midlands, Herefordshire and Worcestershire in summer 1645. Many within the English parliament and army felt that, despite the Scottish contribution of 1644, the civil war had finally been won by the entirely English new model army, not by the Scots. Above all, however, during 1644–5 there were growing religious divisions between the English and Scottish allies.

In 1644 the Scots had sent representatives to the Westminster Assembly, an English-dominated synod set up by the English parliament to advise on a future religious settlement. Established in 1643 to take the heat out of religious differences among English parliamentarians, this body had also been charged with the task of giving substance to the ambiguous religious clause of the Solemn League and Covenant. In 1645 it produced a series of draft documents providing the foundation for a religious settlement for England and Wales, loosely based upon a more presbyterian-type church, though under parliamentary and secular control and shorn of the type of religious independence which the Scottish church enjoyed. The English parliament slowly gave statutory backing to some of the Assembly's recommendations. In practice, however, little attempt was made to establish the new-style church as the sole form of worship. Presbyterian churches seem to have been set up in only a few parts of England and Wales, as one of several alternative forms of Protestant worship available in those areas. Moreover, many English political and military leaders continued roundly to condemn either the presbyterian church itself or any proposal to establish it as the only religion for England and Wales. To many Scots, all this amounted to an English betrayal of God's and the Scottish cause and the terms of their 1643 alliance.

The English civil war ended in summer 1646 when the king surrendered to the Scottish army besieging Newark. On his orders, most remaining royalist bases surrendered, and the Scottish army, with its royal prisoner, pulled back to Newcastle. By this stage Scottish relations with the English parliament had become severely strained. The English parliament, acting as if it alone had won the war, simply wanted rid of the Scots in order to open the way to a purely English settlement. The Scots disliked the radical religious and political views espoused by many English parliamentarians and army officers, and they realised that parliament had no interest in a closer Anglo-Scottish political union or a strict presbyterian church settlement. To add to Scottish gloom, the king was showing no willingness to conclude a deal, either with them or with the English parliament. For the moment cutting their losses and abandoning any hope of reaching a firm settlement with the king or the English parliament, during the opening weeks of 1647 the Scottish army pulled back over the border, accepting an English pay-off and leaving behind Charles I to become a prisoner of the English parliament.

Scotland had chosen to become involved in the British wars of

47

1642–7 in order to pursue British goals. In military terms, the achievement was mixed. A Scottish army succeeded in restoring and retaining control over part of Ireland, but the venture petered out. Scottish forces made a major contribution to turning the tide of the English civil war, but then failed to secure the fruits of unfolding victory; instead, they became sidelined, militarily distracted and politically outmanoeuvred. Largely as a consequence of its involvement in Ireland and England, Scotland also suffered military conflict at home, enduring a campaign falling somewhere between an invasion and a civil war, which brought internal disorder and intense suffering before final victory was achieved. The broader goals lying behind Scottish military involvement in the other two kingdoms remained elusive. In Ireland, the Scots had done little more than consolidate their plantations and religion in a small part of the kingdom; their political influence remained slight. In England, the Scots had been firmly rebuffed, for they had failed either to secure a state church remoulded in the Scottish image or to achieve in practice the closer political, constitutional and military ties which they believed were essential for a durable, stable peace. In this period well over 10,000 Scots had been killed in battle and many more had died of disease or as towns were sacked. The Scots had also endured poor harvests and plague, as well as heavy financial and material demands to support the war effort in three kingdoms. The wars of 1642–7 had been waged at a very high price but had brought the Scots little in return.

Ireland

Initial success in the rebellion of winter 1641–2 had given the Irish Catholics effective political and administrative control over most of Ireland, a control which, although challenged, was largely retained throughout the period 1642–7. They sought a permanent, durable settlement which would in essence make Ireland an autonomous nation under the king, guaranteeing Ireland's political rights and liberties, ensuring that Roman Catholicism would flourish in Ireland unmolested and providing a secure bulwark against both English and Scottish religious interference and the political meddling of the English legislature and executive. Irish Catholic interest in the wars being fought in Scotland and England was limited for, unlike the Scots, the Irish had no serious hope of exerting extensive political influence in, or of exporting their religion to, the other British kingdoms. However, they could neither act in isolation nor avoid being drawn into the British wars. They were threatened by troops which Scotland and England sent to

Ireland in support of Scottish and English personnel and interests there. Moreover, although the potential for direct Irish Catholic involvement in the wars in Scotland and England was never fully realised, it was an important factor in the attitudes towards Ireland adopted by the various power groups in those two kingdoms.

During 1642 the Irish Catholics consolidated their newly won power, encountering limited opposition. Despite the rebels' claims of royal support, Charles roundly condemned them and sought to draw upon Scottish and English resources to restore order in Ireland. However, with his power in both kingdoms now severely limited, there was little that he could do. With the approval and support of the English parliament, during 1642 the Scottish covenanters despatched around 11,000 troops to Ulster to protect Scottish settlers. For a time they succeeded in restoring Protestant control there, but they rarely campaigned outside the province and even within Ulster their influence waned. The English response was weaker, for by autumn 1641 the political nation was already deeply divided, the king lacked the resources to raise an army to fight in Ireland and the English parliament, which might have been able to do so, feared that the army might be hijacked by the king and employed against his enemies in England. By summer 1642 king and parliament were seeking to raise troops to fight in England, not Ireland. During the winter of 1641–2 a little over 1,000 English troops were despatched to Ireland to strengthen the forces in and around Dublin protecting the new English government and fellow-Protestants there. At the same time the Earl of Ormond, appointed by the king lieutenant-general of the forces in Ireland, set about raising additional soldiers among the beleaguered Irish Protestant population.

By the latter half of 1642 the Irish Catholics controlled most of the provinces of Leinster, Munster and Connacht, their troops commanded by experienced officers with continental experience. The Catholic church had come out in support of the rebellion early in 1642 and had organised a series of rebel meetings, culminating in May in a gathering of religious, political and military leaders at Kilkenny. Here was agreed a Catholic confederation of Ireland or the confederation of Kilkenny, by which the Irish Catholics – like the covenanted Scots – bound themselves to work together to achieve common goals, namely the defence of church, crown and liberty. Although loyalty to the king was stressed, the confederates pledged themselves to work for toleration of the Catholic church in Ireland and the supremacy of the Irish parliament. The Kilkenny meeting also established an interim government by a supreme council until a general assembly could meet. The general assembly, a body of Catholic nobility, bishops and elected representatives sitting together in a single chamber, duly gathered at Kilkenny in October 1642. Thereafter the confederates administered Ireland through a hierarchy of central, provincial and county councils, assisted by occasional sessions of the general assembly.

The confederation was, from the outset, an uneasy and imperfect alliance of different Catholic groups. The native Irish had a long history of tribal and provincial separatism, their Catholicism was rooted in papal power, monastic orders and individual priests, and many saw full and open toleration of Catholicism in Ireland as the only basis upon which peace could be built, even if that meant a prolonged estrangement from the king and denying support to Charles in his English wars. The old English, in contrast, had a pedigree of loyalty to the English crown and of helping to rule Ireland in the king's name. They were more open to a Catholicism based upon a regular episcopalian organisation and thus under a degree of potential royal control, and they viewed more favourably the possibility of concluding a compromise deal with the crown which would enable them to return to royal favour and perhaps offer assistance to the king in England. Moreover, some old English held lands taken from the Catholic church at the Reformation, and they feared they might lose them as part of a full restoration of the Catholic church in Ireland. Nevertheless, the confederation held together long enough to consolidate military, political and administrative control over most of Ireland until 1647–8.

Despite initial Catholic successes, at the end of 1642 the Irish Protestants retained or had regained control of much of Ulster, enclaves centred on Dublin and Cork, and a number of isolated towns. Like their Catholic opponents, however, the Protestants in Ireland were deeply divided as well as geographically scattered. There was mutual distrust between the new English and the Scots, personal animosities between the commanders of the various small armies raised to oppose the Catholic threat, and, after the outbreak of civil war in England, growing antipathy between those who sympathised with the king and those who supported the English parliament. Many Protestant troops in the Dublin area tended to support the king and Charles was able to use Dublin-based politicians loyal to him, chiefly Ormond, to gain control over what remained of the new English government. Opponents of the king were purged during 1642–3, and power was increasingly entrusted to Ormond, appointed lord lieutenant of Ireland by the king.

Acting for the king, during 1643 Ormond opened negotiations with the confederate Catholics, looking to conclude a peace with them which would enable many English Protestant troops in Ireland, particularly those in and around Dublin, to be brought over to England to fight for Charles there. The king could not make too many concessions, especially over religion, for fear of alienating his Protestant supporters in England and Ireland. Although falling well short of full Catholic toleration, his offer to continue to enforce anti-Catholic laws in Ireland only very lightly, if at all, did provide the basis for a cease-fire and in September 1643 the king concluded the 'cessation' with the confederate Catholics. A one-year truce, subsequently extended, it recognised Catholic control over most of Ireland while confirming Protestant control over the Dublin and Cork enclaves. It ended fighting in parts of Ireland and enabled the king, during the closing weeks of 1643, to ship back to England over 2,500 troops. Their military impact was limited, for they were roundly defeated by parliamentarian forces in January 1644. Moreover, the fact that the king had done a deal with Irish Catholic rebels and was bringing over to England troops whom the parliamentarians portrayed as Irish Catholics – in fact, they were Protestant soldiers raised in England and Wales – dismayed many royalists and gave valuable propaganda to the English parliament.

Although the cessation continued, further shipments of royalist troops from Ireland to England were limited both by the need to retain a substantial army in Ireland in case the cease-fire collapsed and by the disruption caused by parliamentarian control of the navy and the stationing of a parliamentary fleet in the Irish Sea to prevent such shipments. Pro-parliamentary Protestant forces in Ireland did not recognise or accept the cessation, and new English and Scottish forces continued to fight confederate Catholic troops, especially in parts of Ulster and Munster. There the conflict retained the pattern set more widely before the cessation, of a rather dour, intermittent struggle between garrisons and small locally based armies, of raiding, counter-raiding and small engagements rather than major battles. Something approaching stalemate was reached between the confederate Catholic forces and those Protestant armies which remained active and did not recognise the cessation.

In 1644 the Marquis of Antrim raised 2,000 Catholic troops in Ireland who were despatched to western Scotland and who formed the nucleus of Montrose's army which wreaked such havoc on the Scottish mainland between September 1644 and September 1645. The king saw the potential for employing Irish Catholic troops to turn the tide of the English civil war. From 1644 the king's representatives in Ireland engaged in tortuous negotiations with the confederate Catholics, offering political and religious concessions in return for military aid in England. As before, however, the king's freedom of manoeuvre was limited by fears of losing royalist support in England as well as of undermining royal power in Ireland. Furthermore, Charles's chief negotiator, Ormond, was a firm Protestant and he took a cautious line on religion. In an attempt to break the log-jam, in 1644–5 the king covertly authorised the Earl of Glamorgan, an English Catholic, to negotiate with the confederate Catholics. However, when at the end of 1645 the terms of the deal concluded by Glamorgan were revealed, including complete religious toleration for Catholics in Ireland and possession of all churches not then in Protestant hands, they caused uproar in royalist circles and Charles felt compelled to repudiate them.

Ormond's more cautious negotiations continued during 1645–6 and by March 1646 he was offering a string of concessions – including suspension of penalties for practising Catholicism, admission of Catholics to schools and the legal profession, and the right of Catholics to bear arms and hold military command – in return for an army of 10,000 men to fight for the king in England. Still, however, many Catholics held back from confirming the treaty, arguing that nothing short of explicit royal recognition of the Roman Catholic church, and with it full toleration for Irish Catholics, would suffice. The confederation began to fragment. On the one hand were those, especially the old English, who believed that the king had gone as far as he reasonably could, that the terms on offer should be accepted and that it was in Irish interests to supply military aid to the king in England as a matter of urgency, before the English civil war was completely lost. On the other were those, especially the native Irish, who believed that any deal which fell short of securing full rights for the Roman Catholic church in Ireland was unacceptable. They were bolstered by the hard-line papal nuncio, Giovanni Battista Rinuccini, who had arrived in Ireland in October 1645. By the latter half of 1646 the confederation had split in two, with Rinuccini using military support and the threat of excommunication to overawe the more conciliatory faction. When, as president of a new supreme council, he declared the cessation at an end and made it clear that the Irish Catholics would seek to capture Dublin, many prominent confederate Catholics were appalled and withdrew their support. Ormond, too, appreciated that his cautious attempts to build peace in Ireland acceptable to the king had ended in failure and, rather than see Dublin fall to a hard-line Catholic faction with which there was little chance of the king ever being able to conclude terms, he invited the English parliament to take over and reinforce Dublin in spring 1647.

There was no interlude of peace in Ireland in 1647 as there was in both Scotland and England. However, 1647 does mark a turning point, with the collapse of the confederation and with it any semblance of Irish Catholic unity. In the wake of the 1641 rebellion England and Scotland had strong and direct interests in Ireland, and both intervened in the ensuing military and political power struggle. Scotland sought to impose military control over parts of Ireland, and was itself attacked by a small body of troops raised in Ireland. One side in the English civil war sought to do a deal with the newly dominant force in Ireland which would enable it to employ on the English mainland not only English troops currently stationed in Ireland but also Irish Catholic troops. The other side in the English civil war sought to thwart and negate those plans. In reality, direct Irish involvement in Scotland and England in 1642–7 was limited, not least because the confederate Catholics were seeking not a British settlement but their own Irish settlement, albeit one which would spring from and affect developments in the other British kingdoms. Taking advantage of the distractions suffered by England and Scotland, the confederate Catholics went some way towards achieving their goals, but a durable settlement proved elusive. They met continuing opposition from non-Catholics both inside and outside Ireland and at length their confederation, an uneasy alliance from the outset, began to collapse and turn upon itself. The confederate Catholic achievement of 1642–7 proved incomplete and transitory.

England and Wales

Between 1642 and 1646 England and Wales endured a conflict more intense and prolonged than those which afflicted Ireland and Scotland over the same period, a four-year civil war fought out between two large and equally matched parties. Both sides looked to other parts of the multiple kingdom for support, the royalists to Ireland, the parliamentarians to Scotland. Conversely, during this period England largely shunned direct military involvement in the conflicts in progress in the other two kingdoms. After 1642 few troops were sent to Ireland. The royalists relied on Irish and Scottish, not English troops to challenge covenanter control of Scotland, while the parliamentarians did not give military aid to their Scottish allies on sea or on land, even when the covenanters appeared hard pressed by Montrose. There is no doubting the British overtones of both the causes and consequences of the English civil war, but in its course the war appears largely an English contest which drew military aid from the other two British kingdoms.

During the spring and summer of 1642 parliament in London and the king at York set about creating rival armies. Over the summer Charles and the Earl of Essex, parliament's commander-in-chief, issued commissions to prominent individuals, empowering them to raise regiments. By September both armies were on the move in the West Midlands, eventually clashing at Edgehill in Warwickshire in late October. The battle was indecisive, but in its wake the king may have had an opportunity to march swiftly on London and take the capital. In reality he moved slowly and, by the time he approached the capital in the second week of November, Essex had managed to re-enter London and was reinforced by London's own large and well-equipped militia. Outnumbered, the king withdrew to Oxford, which became the royalists' headquarters for the rest of the war.

As neither side had secured a quick military victory and the conflict seemed likely to continue for the foreseeable future, both sides set about organising for a long war. They raised further troops, most of them forming regional and provincial forces, and attempted to obtain and tie down territory, not only to control key points such as market towns, ports, main roads and major bridges, but also to control the land and population whose resources might supply a continuing war effort. The key means of tying down territory was to garrison it – to place a body of troops in a defendable town, hastily repaired castle, manor house or fortified religious building. In consequence, the ensuing war became marked by raiding, counter-raiding and skirmishing, a regional conflict involving regional armies and commanders, in which major set-piece battles involving the principal or combined armies were the exception. A territorial war of this nature could not easily be decided by a single army or battle, and a prolonged struggle became almost inevitable. Although some towns and counties initially held aloof, during the winter and spring of 1643 attempts to remain neutral and outside the war collapsed or were crushed and most of England and Wales was carved up between royalists and parliamentarians.

It is possible to draw a map of England and Wales in spring 1643 showing the royalists controlling northern England, parts of the West Midlands and the Welsh borders, almost the whole of Wales and the far south-west, with the parliamentarians controlling the rest, including most of the major ports and arsenals of the country. In the course of 1643, however, a string of military victories gave the royalists the upper hand and they advanced on all fronts, sweeping through Yorkshire and Lincolnshire, the western Midlands and southern England, hemming the parliamentarians into London and the south-east, East Anglia and the eastern Midlands, with a vulnerable salient stretching north-westwards. By autumn 1643 the royalists held perhaps two-thirds of England and Wales and were clearly winning the war. Royalist successes might have been greater had they not wasted time and resources in fruitless sieges of the ports of Hull, Plymouth and Gloucester, which parliament managed to relieve by land or by sea. Nevertheless, as the 1643 campaigning season drew towards a close, the royalists were in the ascendant.

During late 1643 and early 1644 the tide turned, in part as a consequence of both sides seeking aid from the other members of the multiple kingdom. The English civil war thus took on a more British hue. Under the terms of the alliance between the English parliament and the Scottish covenanters, during the opening weeks of 1644 a Scottish army of over 20,000 men entered northern England, decisively shifting the balance of power there. The northern royalists, now outnumbered and sandwiched between English and Scottish opponents, gave ground and were forced onto the defensive. The heavy defeat at Marston Moor, near York, on 2 July 1644, followed by a collapse in royalist morale and the departure overseas of several northern royalist commanders, together ensured that by autumn 1644 the north was securely parliamentarian. Whatever its subsequent limitations, in 1644 the Scottish intervention had made a decisive impact. In contrast, the king's truce with the Irish Catholics and his employment in England of several thousand English troops shipped back from the Dublin area probably did the royalist cause more harm than good. It provided ready propaganda for parliament and disturbed many English royalists, while the troops themselves were soon defeated and scattered. However, other factors played a part in the changing fortunes of war in England. There were signs that the English parliamentary war effort was at last proving a match for the victorious but now stretched royalist forces, depleted by the need to garrison newly won territory. The royalist advances in the south and the East Midlands were halted in fairly small but significant battles, at Winceby in October 1643 and at Cheriton in Hampshire in March 1644. It is possible that the availability of economic and material resources also played a part in changing the tide of war, for the royalists – holding generally the less developed and less populous parts of the country – found it progressively harder to maintain a long war effort, while parliament – holding the richest and most thickly populated areas – could better sustain it.

Although the parliamentarians were triumphant in the north during 1644, in large part because of Scottish support, the royalists remained strong in the Midlands and south. If anything, parliamentary standing in those areas fell in 1644, with lacklustre performances in battle and a doomed march by the Earl of Essex deep into the south-west, where his army was trapped by the king and forced to surrender en masse. In consequence, parliament reorganised its forces during the winter of 1644–5, appointing new and more dynamic commanders, including a new commander-in-chief, Sir Thomas Fairfax, and combining several existing armies into a new model army. In co-ordination with other, smaller, parliamentary armies, the new model took the lead in defeating the king's main army at Naseby, Northamptonshire, on 14 June 1645, and in proceeding to mop up most of the remaining royalist forces in the south-west, the West Midlands, the Welsh borderlands and Wales during 1645–6. By spring 1646 the royalist cause was clearly doomed and in May Charles surrendered. Although most surviving royalist strongholds also surrendered during the summer, a few held out in futile isolation to be starved or bombarded into submission during the latter half of 1646 or the opening weeks of 1647. For all practical purposes, however, the civil war in England and Wales ended in early summer 1646 with complete military victory for parliament.

The war imposed enormous strains on England and Wales. Around 100,000 Englishmen and Welshmen were in arms during the campaigning seasons of 1643, 1644 and 1645, and in total perhaps a quarter of a million men served at some point during the civil war. It is estimated that up to 100,000 people were killed as a direct result of military action in England and Wales during 1642–6, and perhaps as many again died from disease and deprivation caused by the war. Some parts of the country, including much of the Midlands, the southern Marches and south-west Wales, suffered intense fighting, as armies rolled backwards and forwards, with attendant killing and material destruction. Other areas largely escaped open war – most of the south-east and East Anglia were held by parliament throughout the war, and most of Wales and the far south-west were firmly royalist for much of the war and then fell quickly and with little bloodshed to parliament. However, nowhere and no one could escape the demands and impact of hostilities. By the latter half of the war both sides were resorting to conscription, impressing unwilling men to serve as well as taking horses and other supplies to maintain their armies. Both sides imposed extremely heavy financial demands, raising huge sums through a mixture of loans, excise duties, the seizure of enemy estates and, heaviest of all, weekly or monthly assessments, a tax on property and income. Traditional local government largely ceased, to be replaced by new royalist or parliamentarian county committees dedicated to squeezing from their counties the money and other resources needed to supply the war effort. These onerous demands were backed by local troops, both field armies and garrisons, which imposed their own burdens through additional local taxes, enforced billeting and plundering. Little wonder that by the closing years of the war there were signs not only of economic exhaustion but also of broad anti-war sentiments. These bubbled to the surface in some areas during 1645–6 in the shape of the 'clubmen', bodies of local men who rose in arms in an attempt to exclude the war and its burdens from their locality or county.

During the civil war the royalists imposed a degree of political control from Oxford, through the role and prerogative powers of the king, the remnants of the privy council, a newly formed council of war and, for a time, the Oxford parliament, comprising members of both Houses whose royalism had led them to quit the Long Parliament in London and to form a separate parliament at Charles's headquarters. The parliamentarians imposed a degree of political control from London, through the depleted Long Parliament itself and a number of central committees, especially the committee of both Houses, expanded and renamed the committee of both kingdoms after it gained some Scottish members early in 1644.

In the course of the war divisions had begun to open up among the leading parliamentary politicians, particularly after the death in December 1643 of John Pym, who had hitherto served as political leader of the parliamentarian cause. In religion, some parliamentarians welcomed the collapse of the Church of England and the emergence during the civil war of different Protestant groups, arguing that they should all be tolerated; others saw this as a high road to heresy and social turmoil and favoured the reimposition of a single state church, either a de-Arminianised Church of England or a church somewhat in the mould of Scottish presbyterianism. In political and constitutional matters, some politicians saw the conflict as vital in curbing royal power and the necessity of pursuing the war to complete military victory in the hope of imposing far-reaching and permanent checks upon the crown; others saw the war as unfortunate and dangerous, opening the way to all sorts of unpleasant and radical ideas, and they favoured reaching a compromise peace with the king at the earliest opportunity, perhaps on the basis of the status quo of 1641.

At one time it was believed that parliamentary politicians divided into two parties – the Independents, who tended to favour pursuing the war to complete victory followed by a sweeping political settlement and broad religious toleration for Protestants, and the Presbyterians, who tended to favour a compromise deal with the king to end the war and to restore most of the pre-war constitution and a single state church. However, most historians now follow in the wake of J.H. Hexter to see a more subtle three-way split, between the doves of the 'peace group', the hawks of the 'war group' and a larger 'middle group' which floated somewhere in between. The king's rejection of the various peace terms put to him by parliament in the course of the war and his determination to fight on scuppered the hopes of the peace party, and the reorganisation of the parliamentary armies and the officer cadre during the winter of 1644–5 was in part a recognition that the civil war would have to be fought to a conclusion and that parliament needed the means to secure a complete military victory. But as war gave way to uneasy peace in 1646–7, the barely concealed differences within the parliamentary cause began to become apparent and ensured that England and Wales, like Scotland and Ireland, would be plunged into further conflict in the late 1640s.

The label 'the English civil war' is a misnomer, and not merely because Wales was caught up in the conflict. Scotland made a large military contribution to the war in England, its intervention in 1644 perhaps decisive in turning the tide of the conflict. The military contribution from Ireland was much smaller and far less influential. As it turned out, the king's attempts to free English troops in Ireland to fight for him in England and to acquire an Irish Catholic army to bolster his English war effort had a greater effect upon events in Ireland than they did upon the course and outcome of the English civil war. In contrast, the intensity of the struggle in England and Wales and the heavy demands it placed upon resources meant that direct English military intervention in either Scotland or Ireland from summer 1642 onwards was very limited. Moreover, the nature of the war in England and Wales – a civil war between two roughly equal parties – the duration and intensity of the contest, and the tendency for the combatants to view it as a separate English and Welsh contest, albeit drawing on British aid, together mark it out as different from the conflicts which unfolded in both Scotland and Ireland during the period.

Conclusion: one war or three?

Between 1642 and 1647 all three British kingdoms endured internal conflicts and wars which were interrelated. In each kingdom the nature, course and outcome of the military contest was to a degree determined by the stances adopted by the other two kingdoms. Montrose's campaign in Scotland in 1644–5 had its foundations in the intervention of a body of Irish troops, was waged in part to support the royalist cause in England, and was greatly helped by the division of the covenanters' resources arising from their involvement in Ireland and England. In Ireland, the Catholic rebels were opposed by Scottish military intervention in Ulster and by very limited English military intervention further south. The Catholic confederation flourished for so long because Scotland and England became distracted by their own wars and because one party in the English civil war successfully sought a truce, and unsuccessfully a full military alliance, in order to boost its prospects within England. In England and Wales both sides sought military aid from the other two British kingdoms, the parliamentarians gaining greatly from an alliance with Scotland, the royalists finding in Ireland, at best, limited military aid which proved double-edged.

Inevitably, perhaps, there were also common features to the experience of war in the three kingdoms. Just as religious strife had helped cause conflict in all three, different religious goals fuelled the war by creating parties willing to wage a bitter and bloody struggle against compatriots. In all three kingdoms major conflict and the need to maintain a substantial war effort brought similar changes to both central and local government and administration, in part designed to place those countries on a war footing and to tap the resources necessary to sustain the war. In all three kingdoms successful military leaders gained a measure of power and influence over political affairs which they would have had no opportunity to exercise in peacetime. In all three kingdoms normal life was dislocated and took on a more military appearance, and all three endured a degree of bloodshed, killing and material destruction which Scotland and Ireland had not suffered since the previous century, and England and Wales not since the Middle Ages.

However, the wars also revealed different levels of British commitment in the three kingdoms. The Scottish covenanters became involved in the Irish and English conflicts in part because they believed successful intervention would bring closer their goal of a durable British political and military settlement built upon federalist principles. Neither the confederate Irish nor the two sides in the English civil war had such strong British perspectives, and their direct military involvement in the wars of the other two kingdoms was always much more limited and grudging than that of the Scots. Various groups in Ireland did enter into negotiations with royalists in England, and engaged in limited military action against covenanters in Scotland, but when the confederate Irish faced the prospect of committing themselves to substantial involvement in the war in England, they balked at the terms and fragmented. The

English royalists and parliamentarians were both keen enough to seek military aid from Scotland and Ireland, but they did so largely to boost their chances of victory in England and to enable them to impose their chosen English settlement on England, not in support of wider British aims. They wished to use British resources to further English, more than British, ambitions.

The nature and time-scale of the wars were also very different in each of the three kingdoms. The Scottish mainland suffered just one year of intensive warfare, associated with the Montrose campaign of 1644–5; for the rest of the period Scots were at war in Ireland and England, but Scotland itself suffered no more than limited pockets of anti-covenanter military activity. Ireland suffered an outburst of bloodletting in the autumn and winter of 1641–2, but thereafter the scale of violence seems to have diminished as the Catholics gained dominance in much of the country. Parts of Ireland endured only low level or sporadic fighting from 1642 onwards, and the cessation of 1643 ensured that many Protestants in Ireland were thenceforth at peace with the Irish Catholics. England and Wales, in contrast, endured an intensive, four-year civil war. Although some parts of the country suffered more harshly and more directly than others, the scale, nature and duration.of the conflict marks out the English civil war as very different from the Scottish and Irish upheavals of the same period.

Given the size, shape and layout of the Atlantic archipelago and the limitations of seventeenth-century transportation, it would have been impossible to wage a single, coherent war ranging across the three British kingdoms. Inevitably, the conflict would have broken down into not merely national but also regional or local theatres – as, indeed, clearly happened during the 1640s in both Ireland and England and Wales, and less clearly in Scotland. Even allowing for this physical reality, however, an analysis of the confrontations and conflicts in progress in Scotland, Ireland, England and Wales between 1642 and 1647 suggests not a common war fought in different theatres, but at least three separate struggles, which assuredly intertwined and influenced each other, and which shared some common causes, features and consequences, but which were also very distinctive and different. The course of the wars in Scotland, Ireland, and England and Wales cannot fully be recounted or understood without an informed appreciation of the ways in which they interwove, but equally the various conflicts waged between 1642 and 1647 cannot plausibly be represented as a single British war fought across three kingdoms.

5

A British military settlement, 1647–51

Introduction: the nature of the settlement

In the years following the English civil war, developments within England and Wales encouraged in each of the three kingdoms not only political fragmentation and realignment but also a royalist military reaction, which was quelled first in England, then in Ireland, and lastly in Scotland. As part of this process the victorious English parliamentary army and its political allies imposed military-backed settlements in each kingdom, driving through a constitutional revolution in England and then launching successful campaigns first to restore in a harsher form traditional English control over Ireland, and then to impose English authority over the hitherto separate kingdom of Scotland. By 1651 the English republic had imposed its dominance over, and a form of union upon, both Ireland and Scotland, and in so doing had moved towards the creation of a more unified British state.

England and Wales

In England and Wales the postwar years were marked by fragmentation within and between parliament and the parliamentary army. Parliamentary politics became dominated by a division between two groups, labelled 'Presbyterians' and 'Independents'. The Presbyterians favoured the re-establishment of royal government with few new restrictions, perhaps even a restoration of the constitutional position of autumn

1641. They also tended to favour the restoration of strict religious discipline imposed through a single state church, thereby ending the religious fragmentation of the war years. The Independents were more suspicious of the defeated king and wished to impose far-reaching new controls over the exercise of royal power. They also tended to favour broad liberty of conscience, welcoming the new Protestant sects and strongly opposing the reimposition of a single state church. During 1646–7 the Presbyterian group gained the upper hand in the House of Commons and began preparations for a settlement with the captive king. Despite Charles's refusal to commit himself, the Presbyterians remained confident that a deal could be struck, but they were aware that they would first have to neutralise the parliamentary army.

In 1646–7 parliamentary forces, up to 50,000 strong, looked to parliament to remedy material and military grievances, including the payment of arrears, an indemnity to prevent prosecution of soldiers for wartime actions and provision for maimed soldiers and military widows and orphans. Many troops had also become imbued with radical Protestant ideas and would therefore oppose any moves by parliament to reimpose a single, potentially intolerant state church. Historians such as Mark Kishlansky and Austin Woolrych differ on how far the soldiers had become radicalised by 1646–7, but it is likely that they were politically aware, keen to ensure that any settlement would provide for religious liberty, prevent a repetition of the breakdown of 1642 and secure the cause for which they had fought. For these very reasons the Presbyterian group in parliament viewed the parliamentary troops as a threat to the type of religious and political settlement which it favoured, and during the opening months of 1647 set about breaking the power of the soldiers. The consequence was a crisis in England caused largely by internal English factors.

Parliament's western army was quietly disbanded but trouble erupted in the late winter and spring when parliament sought to despatch an army of 12,000 to Ireland, to retain a token force of little over 6,000 men in England and Wales, and to disband the rest of the northern and new model armies – over 20,000 men. This was to be accompanied by the payment of little or no arrears and without the other provisions sought by the soldiers. Army unrest grew, particularly within the new model stationed in East Anglia, and military demands gained a slightly broader, political edge, perhaps influenced by the radical political ideas which had sprung up in the wake of the civil war, championed by groups such as the Levellers. The senior officers hesitated but then threw in their lot with the rank and file. During the summer the army seized the political initiative from parliament. A body of troops took custody of the king, who was thereafter a prisoner of the new model army. By the late summer, the officers were negotiating directly with Charles, attempting to reach their own military-backed settlement. The army set out a number of political demands, including the removal of leading Presbyterians from parliament, the dissolution of the Long Parliament and its replacement with fixed-term parliaments, seats in the lower House of which would be redistributed better to mirror the population. Above all, the new model army moved physically closer to London as an implied threat to parliament; in August it even temporarily entered the capital to crush pro-Presbyterian mob pressure on parliament.

Although for the moment the Presbyterian group in parliament had been cowed and parliament's anti-army activities checked, the army's enhanced position itself encouraged divisions to open up within it. Senior officers, many of them worried by the radical political ideas spreading among the rank and file, attempted swiftly to reach a settlement with the king on the basis of a new document, the Heads of the Proposals, which took a moderately Independent line by envisaging broad religious toleration, temporary controls over the military, judicial and executive powers of the king, and lenient treatment for former royalists, as well as fixed-term biennial parliaments. Many rank and file soldiers viewed their officers with growing suspicion and the Heads of the Proposals as too soft. Instead, they prepared their own, more radical terms for a settlement, the Agreement of the People, which stressed that power lay with the people and their elected representatives, implying that the crown and House of Lords possessed little power, and asserted that the people had certain inalienable rights, including religious liberty and equality before the law. In debates held between senior officers and representatives of the rank and file at Putney in late October and early November, it became clear that the army was deeply divided and that radical, Leveller ideas, anathema to senior officers and much of the political elite, had gained a strong hold within the army.

Charles had declined to accept any of the settlements offered by English political and military groups, in part because he was encouraged by the spectacle of his English opponents falling out among themselves, in part because he was angling for a military alliance with the Scots. He escaped from Hampton Court in November 1647 and, although he got no further than renewed captivity on the Isle of Wight, from there he concluded an agreement with the Scots in the closing week of 1647. His flight and subsequent Scottish alliance threatened a renewed military challenge to parliamentary control of England and Wales, but also helped reunite the parliamentary army to face that threat. The senior officers reimposed control, easily crushing a half-hearted mutiny, holding the army back from any immediate challenge to the Long Parliament but supporting a hardening attitude against the king.

The year 1648 was marked by riots, risings and rebellions in many parts of England and Wales, including Cornwall, Surrey, Kent, parts of East Anglia, Yorkshire, north-west Wales and much of south Wales, largely caused by English and Welsh factors, though also encouraged by news of the Scottish royalist alliance. In part, they sprang from attempts by royalists to reverse the first civil war and to restore royal power through arms. In part, they fed upon social and economic difficulties, for 1647–8 were years of bad weather, poor harvests, high prices and high unemployment. But they also drew upon a broader disillusionment, shared by former parliamentarians and royalists. Although the civil war had ended in 1646, little progress had been made towards restoring traditional, civilian local government and pre-war low taxation. Instead, the semi-military local government of the war years continued, taxes remained high, there was still a very strong military presence and, in the wake of the effective collapse of the Church of England during the civil war, little had been done to re-establish religious order, while a whole range of ideas and sects, which many viewed as heretical, were flourishing unchecked.

Together, these differing grievances and aspirations provoked widespread disturbances during the spring and summer. Most were contained by locally based army units. Two were more serious. One began in Kent but crossed into Essex, culminating in a long siege of rebel-held Colchester by part of the new model army under Fairfax. The other, a rising in south Wales, was checked by local forces in May but culminated in a long siege of rebel-held Pembroke by another part of the new model under Cromwell. It was fortunate for the English parliamentarians that the planned Scottish royalist invasion of England took so long to prepare that by the time the Scots crossed the border most of the home-grown disturbances had been crushed and Pembroke was about to fall. This allowed Cromwell to lead much of the new model army north, gathering reinforcements en route, and to concentrate upon engaging the Scots. With the defeat of the Scottish army at Preston in mid-August and the fall of most rebel-held outposts, the war was over.

The experience of fighting and winning a second civil war hardened attitudes within the army, which swept on during the closing weeks of 1648 to seize control of the political agenda. Angered by parliament's continued willingness not only to negotiate with the king but also to contemplate his restoration to power with few preconditions, the army entered London in early December and purged from the Commons all MPs believed to be inclined to treat with Charles or hostile to the army. A rump of less than eighty remained active in the House. Acting in league with the army and ignoring the moribund House of Lords, these proceeded during the opening weeks of 1649 to set up a high court to try the king for treason and, after Charles's execution, formally to abolish monarchy in England, Wales and Ireland, to abolish the House of Lords and to establish England and Wales as 'a Commonwealth and Free State'. The failure of the Rump – as this remnant of the Long Parliament was soon dubbed – to enact domestic reforms and to prepare a new constitutional settlement eventually alienated the army. However, in the shorter term, and working in harmony with the English army, the Rump authorised and supported major campaigns from 1649 to reconquer Ireland and from 1650 to conquer Scotland. Both were successful and led to a process of union and incomplete assimilation. During the 1650s the new English republic created a militarised and Anglocentric British republic.

In 1647 various power groups within the English political nation had attempted unsuccessfully to construct a firm and durable settlement. Although Scotland had helped the English parliament to win the war, the projected settlements were almost exclusively English. The Heads of the Proposals was a partial exception, for it did call for the confirmation of Anglo-Scottish treaties and the appointment of conservators of the peace between the two nations, though other clauses cut across Scottish religious aspirations and undermined earlier Anglo-Scottish agreements. The king's refusal to accept any of these projected settlements, caused in part by his hopes of Scottish aid, encouraged growing unrest and helped provoke a second civil war, though the renewed violence of 1648 sprang in large part from internal English and Welsh discontent. The seizure of power by the parliamentary army in the wake of that war and the settlement which it imposed upon England produced a hostile reaction in Scotland and Ireland, but it also enabled the new English republic to adopt a much more dynamic and aggressive approach to the other two British kingdoms and to force through an English-led British military settlement, largely complete by 1651. Developments within England, in which Ireland and Scotland took an interest but which were largely beyond their influence, had prepared the ground for English hegemony of the Atlantic archipelago.

Ireland

During 1647–8 the departure of the remnants of Munro's Ulster army ended Scottish military involvement in Ireland. The victorious English parliament had appointed a new lord lieutenant of Ireland in 1646 and for a time had contemplated launching a major campaign to recover control of the country, but when Lord Lisle eventually arrived in February 1647 he brought with him few troops and little money. He soon departed, having made little impact beyond antagonising several of the anti-confederate political and military leaders. However, the English parliament did seize the opportunity offered by Ormond in spring 1647 to take control of the Dublin area, and in June Michael Jones landed with an English army of 2,000 men to defend the Irish capital. On 8 August he engaged and destroyed a confederate Catholic army at Dungan Hill, near Trim, so relieving Dublin. At the same time the Earl of Inchiquin, a native Irishman but a firm Protestant and an opponent of the confederation, re-established control over parts of the south, capturing the towns of Dungarvan in May and Cashel in September, and routing a confederate army at Knocknanuss near Mallow on 13 November.

These military disasters undermined the position of those within the confederation – chiefly the more radical native Irish and the group loyal to the papal nuncio, Rinuccini – who had rejected the proposed treaty with Ormond and the royalists in 1646, ended the cessation and renewed military activity. Conversely, they greatly strengthened the hands of the more cautious old English who now took control. Resuming their search for a compromise deal which would bring peace to Ireland, they opened negotiations with Inchiquin which led to a formal truce in May 1648. Rinuccini condemned both negotiations and truce, but his star was clearly on the wane. His closest ally, Owen Roe O'Neill, led his native Irish Ulster army south to threaten the confederate capital of Kilkenny, but he lacked the will and perhaps the power to push home an attack and instead himself concluded a truce with Inchiquin and withdrew.

The renewed civil war in England and Wales in 1648 and the king's Scottish alliance caused a realignment within Ireland. The new English Protestants of Dublin were largely parliamentarian in sympathy and the region was dominated by pro-parliamentary troops. The Munster Protestants were divided, especially when Inchiquin declared for the king in April 1648. Most Ulster Scots tended towards the royalism then dominant on the Scottish mainland, though pro-parliamentary troops under George Monck moved quickly to secure key garrisons and limit the Scots' capacity to cause disruption. Many of the Irish Catholics also sympathised with the plight of Charles I, but the uncertainties of 1644–6 re-emerged, with many Catholics still feeling that they could not actively support the king until he had firmly pledged support for full toleration of Roman Catholicism in Ireland.

The king's Irish linchpin, Ormond, landed in southern Ireland in September 1648, seeking to mobilise pro-royalist groups in Ireland, both Catholic and Protestant. Inchiquin gave him support and in January 1649 the confederate Catholics also concluded a treaty with him, the now dominant old English accepting terms very similar to those offered by Ormond in March 1646, even though they fell short of securing full rights for the Catholic church in Ireland. With the king defeated in England and facing trial and execution, many Catholic church leaders also now accepted these terms, though others held aloof. In Ulster, O'Neill rejected the alliance and instead concluded a truce with parliamentary forces in the province. The Ulster Scots were divided, for although many had reservations about the new English regime, only some actively supported Ormond's open royalism and most declined to commit themselves. English parliamentary forces, particularly those under Jones, in and around Dublin, opposed Ormond's royalist alliance and began preparing for an expected Irish royalist offensive.

The 'Ormondists' – supporters of this Irish royalist alliance – opened their campaign in June 1649. Inchiquin captured the towns of Drogheda, Dundalk, Newry and Trim, while Ormond advanced on Dublin. However, on 2 August Michael Jones, recently reinforced by a further batch of 2,600 English troops, engaged and routed Ormond at Rathmines. By that time the new English republic had already committed itself to a major campaign to regain control of Ireland, aimed at restoring order and English dominance, protecting Protestant interests in Ireland, preventing Ireland from being used as a launching pad for a royalist invasion of England and placing Irish land at English disposal. In 1642 the English parliament had earmarked two million acres of Irish land, to be confiscated from the rebels and redistributed to those who loaned money to finance an English campaign there, and by 1649 the English regime was anxious to seize Irish land to pay off a range of creditors. About 12,000 men from the English parliamentary army were shipped to Dublin in August under the command of Cromwell, to join the 8,000 or so troops already there. Jones's victory at Rathmines ensured that Cromwell landed unopposed in a now safe enclave around Dublin, and had a secure base.

Between September 1649 and May 1650 Cromwell re-established firm English military control over much of eastern and southern Ireland. Having captured the strongly defended town and port of Drogheda, north of Dublin, in September 1649, Cromwell sent a detached force under Robert Venables and Charles Coote to mop up Ulster. In response, in October O'Neill tardily threw in his lot with Ormond, but he was already very ill and after his death on 6 November the native Irish of Ulster lacked a dynamic and experienced military leader to defend them against the English parliamentary army. Coote and Venables were able to break continuing resistance in Ulster, routing what remained of the native Irish Ulster army at Scarrifhollis near Letterkenny in June 1650. The Ulster Scots had generally not resisted the English parliamentarians and by spring 1650 many were actively supporting them. Cromwell, meanwhile, had turned his attention south, capturing much of Leinster. A Protestant resurgence in Munster, led by Lord Broghill, ensured that many of its towns were opened to the parliamentarians unopposed.

Cromwell left Ireland in May 1650, having broken resistance in three of the four provinces. He was replaced by his son-in-law, Henry Ireton, who by the end of the year had taken all the strongholds of Ulster, Leinster and Munster. Despairing of an Irish route back to the English crown, in summer 1650 the late king's son, styling himself Charles II, concluded a treaty with the Scots. As part of the deal he was forced to renounce and condemn Ormond's 1649 treaty with the confederate Irish – because of the antipathy between the Scottish presbyterians and the Irish Catholics, he could not maintain an alliance with both and had to choose between them. Most surviving Irish Catholic forces now rejected the leadership of Ormond, for not only had he brought military defeat but also he could no longer deliver royal concessions on religion. Ormond and many of the remaining anti-parliamentarian leaders, including Inchiquin, left Ireland at the end of the year. Ireton consolidated English control during 1651, overrunning County Clare and capturing Limerick. His death late in 1651 did not halt the English advance, for during 1652 most of Connacht, including Galway, fell to parliament and many of the remaining Irish Catholic guerrilla forces surrendered.

By 1652–3 English control over Ireland had been restored and the English republic proceeded to cement its authority, installing an English military and civilian administration in Dublin, stationing a large part of the parliamentary army – at times, over 30,000 men – in Ireland, tying Ireland more closely to English political control, and passing legislation which underlined English dominance of Ireland and dispossessed Irish Catholics, especially the native Irish. Most native Irish in Ulster, Leinster and Munster lost their property and were transplanted to Connacht, and huge tracts of Irish land were made available to those who had invested in the war effort, and to other civilian and military creditors of the English regime. After a decade or more of rebellion, war, plague and famine, which had devastated the Irish population, English authority over Ireland had been restored through military force. It led on to a curbing of Irish rights and liberties, to a much tighter form of English control over Ireland than during the pre-war decades, and to transplantation of the native Irish population and a massive redistribution of property which together ensured that, by the latter half of the 1650s, probably no more than 20 per cent of Irish land remained in Catholic hands.

With a long record of English control over Ireland there was never any possibility that the English regime would allow the Irish to go their own way. Throughout the period 1647–51 the English regime was intervening directly and militarily in Ireland, at first to prevent the complete collapse of English authority there, and then, once English distractions were at an end, to mount a full-scale reconquest of the whole nation. This was followed by a resumption of English control, bolstered by a massive redistribution of land which fundamentally altered the social, economic and religious balance within Ireland. Although many of the developments within Ireland over this period had roots in the unresolved Irish divisions and tensions – among both Catholics and Protestants – in the years following the Irish rebellion they were in turn provoked, sharpened, redirected and resolved by developments in England, with attempts in Ireland both to take advantage of divisions within England in 1647–8 and to rally to the aid of the royalist cause in England and Ireland in the years 1648–51. They reaped a bitter harvest. In 1641 the Irish Catholics had rebelled to enhance and secure Irish political and religious liberties. But they had helped trigger developments in England which produced a regime even more hostile to Irish Catholic interests and which resulted in the crushing and dispossession of Irish Catholics.

Scotland

The Scottish covenanters' involvement in the English civil war of 1642–6 had not brought about the broader British settlement which they sought, and during 1647–8 it became starkly apparent that the English parliament had no interest in such a settlement. It largely ignored the British clauses of the 1641 treaty of London and the 1643 Solemn League and Covenant, unilaterally ended Scottish representation on the committee of both kingdoms and, without consulting the Scots, appointed a new English lord lieutenant of Ireland. Above all, the English parliament and army engaged in negotiations to reach an English political, constitutional and religious settlement with the defeated king, apparently ignoring Scotland. Disappointment, disillusionment and fear produced a reaction in Scotland during 1647.

Scottish royalists wished to aid Charles I and, led by Hamilton, they encouraged wider Scottish support. Opponents of the covenanters saw an opportunity to curb covenanter power. Moreover, many moderate covenanters themselves came to see a virtue in supporting Charles, either because they wished to help their king at a time when he was being treated dishonourably by the English, or because they now viewed a chastened king as a better vehicle for securing their British goals than the English parliament and army. After tortuous negotiations involving the king, who, although a prisoner, was able to negotiate via courtiers allowed access to him, Charles concluded a deal with the Scots – 'the engagement' – in December 1647. He pledged to support the 1641 Scottish settlement, including the British elements of the treaty of London, so bringing about closer Anglo-Scottish political, commercial and diplomatic co-operation, and to enforce presbyterianism as the sole religion of England and Wales for a trial period of three years. In return, the Scots were to restore him to full power in England and Ireland, if necessary by force and by calling upon English and Irish assistance. The engagement, like earlier Scottish treaties and alliances, was a three-kingdoms document. In reality not all Scots supported the engagement. Hardliners felt that the offer to establish presbyterianism in England and Wales for a temporary period only was unacceptable and, in any case, many believed that Charles could not be trusted to do even this.

Many covenanters, including politicians like Argyll, the general assembly and elements within the scaled-down covenanter army, held aloof from the deal. However, the Scottish parliament supported the engagement and, despite some opposition, the engagers managed to raise an army of around 20,000 during the spring and summer of 1648. Most of this engager army entered England during the second week of July, seeking to link up with English and Welsh royalists. But by July most of the pro-royalist and anti-parliamentarian risings in England and Wales had been crushed or contained, and the Scottish army attracted little support in northern England. It was also poorly led and encountered appalling weather. On 17 August parliamentary forces under Cromwell shattered much of this army at Preston and surviving elements were mopped up in southern Lancashire. Many prominent engagers were killed in battle or, like Hamilton, were captured and executed by the English.

In the wake of this defeat, engager power in Scotland collapsed. In September 1648, in the so-called 'whiggamore raid', a covenanter force drawn from south-west Scotland – a region of strict and radical presbyterianism – ejected engager political leaders from Edinburgh and ensured their replacement by a strict covenanter government. Cromwell and much of his army entered Scotland unopposed in October and lent support to this new government under Argyll. Cromwell was content to have politicians with whom he believed he could work back in power in Scotland, and was relieved that he would not have to fight a nation of fellow-Protestants. The covenanters purged engagers and other former royalists from government and the army and, working closely with the presbyterian church, embarked on a programme of moral and administrative reform. With so many of the elite now barred from office the new regime took on a socially less elevated and more radical appearance.

The execution of the king again changed the direction of Scottish politics. Whatever their differing allegiances during the 1640s, many Scots were deeply shocked that their king had been killed by the English without Scottish consultation. The English parliament then abolished monarchy in England, Wales and Ireland, though it remained silent about the situation in Scotland, apparently happy to let the Scots go their own way. Far from winning closer political and religious union, the Scots now saw that even the Anglo-Scottish regal union had been severed. However, the Scots were not prepared to accept this unilateral solution. In February 1649 Charles I's eldest son was proclaimed by the Scottish covenanter government king of 'Great Britain' – of England and Scotland – and Ireland. This ended the tense relationship between the restored covenanter regime and the parliamentary cause, for the new English republic rightly interpreted it as a direct challenge.

The cause of Charles II divided the Scottish political nation. In exile on the continent, Charles showed little love for the covenanters and long held aloof, apparently seeing Ireland as a better route to recover England. He dragged his heels in negotiations with Scottish representatives and was suspected of complicity in a short-lived royalist campaign, waged by foreign mercenaries under Montrose, in the far north of Scotland in spring 1650. This ended in defeat at Carbisdale on 27 April 1650 and Montrose's execution. By the opening months of 1650 it was clear that the English republic was restoring control over Ireland, and Charles looked more seriously to Scotland as a vehicle for regaining England. In

71

June 1650 he grudgingly took the two covenants as the price of winning Scottish support. Even so, when Charles arrived in Scotland shortly afterwards he was viewed with suspicion by many covenanters, who sought to control him and keep him away from the capital, the army and pro-royalist enclaves in the north.

It is unclear whether Charles and his Scottish royalist colleagues ever seriously intended to honour their deal with the Scottish covenanters. Certainly, many strict covenanters viewed Charles as untrustworthy and the alliance with him as ungodly and doomed, a few even suggesting that the interests of the Scottish nation and church might be better served by reaching a compromise political settlement with the English republic. Such views were particularly strongly held in the south-west, which had raised its own separate army to defend covenanter ideals and which, in October 1650, issued a remonstrance criticising the deal struck with Charles II and suggesting that the Scots had no right to impose their king on England. However, many moderate covenanters, though aware of the risks, now saw support for the king as the best means of securing an honourable and durable settlement on Scottish terms. Scottish royalists and other anti-covenanter groups generally favoured helping Charles almost unconditionally. In December 1650 the pro-royalist covenanter majority issued a resolution, allowing royalists, including former engagers and supporters of Montrose, to join the covenanter army, broadening it into an 'army of the kingdom'. This sparked a formal protest in the south-west. Even in the face of an English army of invasion, the Scots were disintegrating into parties – 'remonstrants', 'resolutioners' and 'protesters'.

Although it had been distracted by the need to restore control over Ireland, by summer 1650 the English republic was prepared to meet the Scottish threat enunciated by the proclamation of Charles II as king of Great Britain and reinforced by Scottish military preparations. Rather than await a Scottish invasion, in July Cromwell led an army of 16,000 men into Scotland. The refusal of the Scottish army to give battle and its ability to fall back behind heavily defended lines around Edinburgh frustrated Cromwell, and by early September his disease-ravaged forces were threatened by Leslie's much larger Scottish army at Dunbar. However, on 3 September Cromwell secured a stunning and unexpected victory in battle which opened to him most of the lowlands, including Edinburgh and Glasgow. Two months later part of Cromwell's army defeated the separate south-western Scottish army outside Hamilton – although estranged from the main covenanter cause, these forces somewhat tardily took the field against an English conquest.

However, the English campaign then became bogged down, in part because Cromwell suffered prolonged illness, in part by the inability of the English army to challenge the covenanter forces in the highland zone. Leslie had retreated there to rebuild his army, with Stirling as his new headquarters. Not until summer 1651 was the stalemate broken, when Cromwell shipped most of his troops across the Firth of Forth, his bridgehead secured by victory over part of Leslie's army at Inverkeithing in late July. With the English now threatening his supply lines to the highlands, but with few of them left in southern Scotland, Leslie and Charles II – who had been formally crowned at Scone in January – seized the opportunity to lead the Scottish army, initially up to 20,000 strong, south into England. Cromwell, probably expecting such a move, pursued it to Worcester, where he defeated and destroyed it on 3 September.

Around 6,000 English troops under George Monck had been left in Scotland to mop up. They quickly captured Stirling and Dundee, and by the end of 1651 most open resistance was at an end. The English republic moved to cement the military victory by placing Scotland under English rule. The Scottish parliament and general assembly were abolished, an English administration was installed in Edinburgh, an English army of over 10,000 men was stationed in Scotland and new fortresses were built to underscore English military control. The English regime also passed laws and ordinances to formalise the union of Scotland with a dominant England and to bring Scotland into line with English practice, and a degree of English-style religious liberty was forced on Scotland with *de facto* toleration for non-presbyterian Protestant groups. The Scottish dream of a federal union on Scottish terms had turned into the reality of an enforced union with England on English terms.

In the period 1647–51 Scotland may have had the opportunity to reach its own purely Scottish settlement, royalist or non-royalist. The English parliamentary regime indicated that it was interested in an English and Irish settlement, either with Charles I or on republican principles, and it might have been content to let Scotland go its own way. However, almost without exception the factions comprising the Scottish political nation found this unacceptable, either because they remained true to their belief that only a British settlement on Scottish terms would prove durable, or because they now supported the royalist cause and wished to see their king restored to full power in England. Many viewed these two objectives as compatible and mutually supporting, though some covenanters had their doubts, and it is a moot point whether Charles I or Charles

II ever truly accepted the goal of a British settlement. Events in Scotland were shaped by those in England, as the Scots repeatedly reacted to developments which the English apparently thought did not concern them – the attempt to reach a purely English settlement after 1646, English treatment of the king, the divisions and renewed war in England in 1648, the execution of Charles I, the abolition of monarchy and the English conquest of Ireland. Repeated Scottish interference in areas which the English regime felt did not concern them eventually convinced the English republic that a long-cherished Scottish objective was correct – that only closer Anglo-Scottish links could deliver a durable peace. However, when it occurred it was not based on a negotiated settlement on Scottish terms, but on the English regime's conquest and attempted assimilation of its northern neighbour.

Conclusion: one settlement or three?

The three kingdoms shared several common features in the period 1647–51. In all three, old unresolved difficulties and new problems together caused a fragmentation of existing power groups – the parliamentarians in England and Wales, the confederate Catholics in Ireland and the covenanters in Scotland – and their realignment in new alliances. In England and Wales the alliances were between royalists and disillusioned parliamentarians in 1648, and thereafter between the parliamentary army and its allies against the rest, in Ireland between royalists and moderate confederate Catholics, in Scotland between royalists and moderate covenanters. In all three, these new divisions and alliances fuelled continuing or renewed warfare.

It is also clear that developments in each nation continued to depend to varying degrees upon events in one or both of the other British kingdoms. There was some interaction between Scottish and Irish events in this period – Charles II's desertion of Ormond in Ireland in summer 1650 because of his need to conclude a Scottish alliance, for example – but it was more limited than in the earlier periods. In contrast, the Scots were profoundly affected by developments in England. Their exclusion from the projected English settlement of 1647–8 and from the punishment of their king in January 1649 produced two royalist reactions in Scotland. The first led to a failed invasion of England in 1648, trailing in its wake an internal realignment of Scottish politics, the second to a successful English invasion of Scotland, another failed Scottish invasion of England and an enforced and unequal union. The situation in Ireland was also influenced by English divisions and renewed civil war down to

1648, and by English treatment of the king of Ireland. Again, this produced a reaction in favour of the royalist cause in 1648–9 which provoked a successful English military invasion of Ireland and an enforced union. From England's perspective, the refusal of Charles I to reach a settlement with any faction during 1647 was caused, in part, by the availability of Scottish support for his cause, just as potentially the most serious threat to the English parliament in 1648 was the Scottish royalist invasion. Although it did not lead to an invasion of the English and Welsh mainland, the royalist reaction in Ireland rendered the Irish, as much as the Scots, a continuing threat to the new English regime, so stirring the new English republican regime to invade, conquer and control Ireland and Scotland.

However, after 1647 these interrelationships between the three kingdoms become much looser and less equal. England was setting the agenda, and most key developments in Scotland and Ireland, including the political realignments and military initiatives there, were responses to events which occurred in England. The English initially sought a settlement focused largely or entirely upon England and Wales, but the attempt provoked strong reactions in Scotland and Ireland. It seems likely that the English parliamentarians always intended to restore England's traditional control over Ireland, though it was largely English developments which determined the timing and nature of that restoration. It is possible that the English parliamentary cause intended to let Scotland go its own way, and was unwillingly compelled to flex its muscles there only because of an unhelpful Scottish reaction.

Above all, although the English parliamentary army and its political allies eventually imposed a settlement on all three nations, it took a different form in each. In England there was a military coup, but one leaving a semblance of existing political forms intact and involving no great social or economic upheaval. Scotland suffered a military conquest leading to an enforced union, but one which respected the basic rights of much of the native population, did not involve significant colonisation by non–Scots and was quite easily reversed at the restoration. In Ireland a more brutal military conquest led to an enforced union which dispossessed much of the native population, and which took the form of a mixture of ethnic cleansing and an assault on the majority religion. This fundamentally altered the Irish tenurial and religious balance, profoundly affecting the history of that country for centuries to come. In Ireland, at least, the legacy of the British wars still lurks near the surface.

6

Conclusions: a common experience?

Although 'New British History' is still in its infancy, historians such as Nicholas Canny, Keith Brown and David Cannadine have taken a sceptical or critical view of the fledgling. First, it is argued that most studies which treat developments within the three kingdoms as parts of a single, common process have taken a fairly narrow political approach, focusing on politics, the constitution and state religion, while ignoring or greatly underplaying social and economic history, demography, environmental history, commerce, linguistic developments and so on. This is certainly true of most attempts to draw together a British history of the mid-seventeenth century. Second, it is claimed that much so-called British history is, in reality, simply an attempt more fully to explain English developments through an expanded awareness of how Scottish and Irish factors influenced England, thus retaining a firm Anglocentric focus, rather than providing a balanced attempt to trace the development of each kingdom and the ways in which they interacted with each other. A very detailed published study of the 'British' crisis of 1637–42, Russell's *The Fall of the British Monarchies*, has attracted criticism on precisely these grounds. Third, British history is alleged to exaggerate the unity and integrity of the component kingdoms and to underplay internal divisions. Accordingly it is suggested that, for many periods, including the crises and conflicts of the mid-seventeenth century, it would be more accurate and informative to adopt a local and provincial rather than national and British approach, or to focus on internal divisions between the highland and lowland zones in Scotland and in England and Wales,

76

and between the relatively fertile and infertile zones in Ireland. Fourth, it is claimed that much British history underplays or ignores links which the three kingdoms had with the continent of Europe and continental influences in British history. In fact, such influences were not strong in the mid-seventeenth-century British conflict, for much of the continent was absorbed by the later stages of the Thirty Years War and then a continuing Franco-Spanish conflict. Although many British officers had acquired military experience fighting as mercenaries on the continent, there was little direct continental military intervention in the British wars. Fifth, it is suggested that it may be beyond the powers of a single historian to possess or to acquire the deep, specialist knowledge of all three kingdoms needed to write a full and balanced British account and that, in any case, as far less work has been undertaken on Scotland and Ireland than on England, the priority should be for much more specialist research on Scottish and Irish aspects before we are in a position to synthesise material into a British account. In terms of the mid-seventeenth century it is certainly true that far less research has been conducted on Scotland and Ireland than on England.

Despite these objections, historians such as Morrill, Pocock and – to a degree – Russell suggest that the wars of the mid-seventeenth century were sufficiently interrelated to be viewed as components of a British phenomenon. Such historians suggest that one or more common roots lay at the heart of the various crises and conflicts which occurred within and between Scotland, Ireland, and England and Wales from the late 1630s to the early 1650s, and that both the course and the outcome of those conflicts were crucially shaped by their development within the context of a multiple kingdom. Accordingly some historians now see a British perspective as a – perhaps the – vital analytical channel which will lead to a full understanding and appreciation of the causes, course and consequences of the conflicts of 1637–51. For such historians these conflicts are best described, with varying degrees of caution, as 'the war of the three kingdoms', 'the wars of the three kingdoms', 'the war(s) of the three kingdoms' or 'the British wars'.

There is no doubt that the conflicts of the mid-seventeenth century within and between the three kingdoms were closely interconnected and shared many common features. Time and again one kingdom reacted to, or copied, developments in another. For example, the rebellion of the Irish Catholics in 1641 was in part a reaction to the policies of the newly dominant Scottish covenanters, in part an attempt to win for Ireland the same type of liberties which the covenanters had successfully secured for Scotland. Again, the English Triennial Act of 1641 may have been modelled on the Scottish triennial provision of the previous year, just as the Irish parliament's revival of impeachment in 1641 may have been triggered by the English parliament's use of that procedure in 1640–1. Time and again, common features can be identified in all three kingdoms. For example, it is possible to explain the crises, descents into conflict and wars of the late 1630s and early to mid-1640s in all three kingdoms as reactions to the rule of the untrustworthy, authoritarian and interventionist Charles I – the king was, after all, one of the few points of contact affecting all three – just as the crises and wars of the late 1640s and beyond can be portrayed as a three-kingdom reaction against the English parliamentary regime and its army. Equally, it is possible to suggest that religious fears and divisions proved the principal force in driving all three nations to take up arms, and that the ensuing conflicts in all three kingdoms were variants on a common British war of religion. Some historians, such as Ronald Hutton, have argued that the principal consequence of these conflicts, namely the enforced British union of the 1650s and the incorporation of Scotland and Ireland with England, created or secured English political and military superiority within Britain which, despite the renewed division following the restoration, thereby established the balance and relationship between the three kingdoms which prevailed for much of the modern era. In short, it is clear that there was close interplay between the three kingdoms in the mid-seventeenth century, that developments within any one can only fully be understood if its relationship with the other two is considered, and that events in each would not have unfolded when and how they did if it had stood in isolation rather than as a member of a multiple kingdom.

However, even historians such as Pocock, who are sympathetic to this approach, point out that there were significant differences between the three kingdoms. For example, they endured different types of war. England suffered a civil war between two groups who were drawn from a single polity and who shared the same religion, and then went on to fight to regain control of Ireland and, as an unwelcome consequence of Scottish actions, to conquer and incorporate Scotland as well. Scotland suffered a limited degree of civil war in 1644–5 with Montrose's campaigns, and again in 1648–51 between engagers and non-engagers, but from the outset the dominant covenanters adopted a British policy which encompassed England and Ireland. It was, though, a policy resting in large part on a desire better to secure newly won Scottish rights and autonomy, and one which eventually led to invasion and incorporation. Ireland endured a mixture of civil war between Irishmen of the same religion and culture and internal conflict between different racial and religious groups who lived in Ireland, again in part spurred on by the desire of some to secure greater Irish rights and autonomy, and again leading to invasion and incorporation.

The manner in which these wars were waged was also different. With a few exceptions the war in England and Wales was reasonably civilised, and killings were kept to a minimum, but Scotland suffered more brutal campaigns, especially those associated with Montrose in 1644–5, while Ireland endured both internal conflicts and foreign invasions that were often extremely brutal and bloody, with slaughter aplenty. The numbers fighting in each kingdom differed greatly, though when viewed as relative to the resident population of each kingdom the differences are not so great. At the height of the three-kingdom conflict, in the early to mid-1640s, there were generally 100,000 or more men in arms in England and Wales during the campaigning season (out of a population of a little over five million), generally fewer than 50,000 in arms in Ireland (which had a population of over a million, perhaps nearer two million according to some estimates) and, even during Montrose's campaign, fewer than 20,000 in arms in Scotland (which probably had a population of less than one million).

The consequences of the wars also differed from country to country. One of the principal results of the war in England and Wales was the spread of a range of new, radical political and religious ideas, disseminated through a booming and uncensored press and fairly well-organised groups and sects. For a number of reasons, including the continued dominance of Scotland and Ireland by well-established churches, the continuing power of the landed elite, a weaker press and a smaller urban sector, such strong and overt radical activity was not a feature of Scotland and Ireland in the 1640s, though radical ideas were carried there by the English parliamentary army when stationed in both countries in the 1650s. Such examples could be multiplied many times over to demonstrate marked differences between the three kingdoms.

There is a danger that attempts to pull things together into an overall conclusion will seek to be all-encompassing to the point of blandness, suggesting that the British wars amounted to more (or less) than one single war, but less (or more) than three separate wars, that the conflicts comprised both a war of the three kingdoms and at the same time a series of self-contained wars, and, turning to the views of contemporaries, that some saw one British war fought over three kingdoms, others three interlocking but essentially different national wars, and others again a series of largely local or regional conflicts. Although the wars which broke out in Scotland, Ireland, England and Wales can be interpreted as manifestations of a common British malady, such as a reaction against Charles I or royal religious innovation, they can also be seen as arising separately for reasons which were largely internal and peculiar to each kingdom, though its place within a multiple kingdom ensured that in each case fighting the war and concluding the postwar settlement brought that kingdom into close contact with one or both of its neighbours.

Certainly in this period, as in any other, each kingdom had its own separate and distinct history, in many respects quite different from those of its two British neighbours. Attempts to explain the causes, course and consequences of the wars in any one kingdom must, therefore, range over political, constitutional, religious, social, economic or cultural factors, many of them peculiar to that kingdom; it is most unlikely that a full explanation can be found by focusing upon 'the British problem' or the problems of a 'multiple kingdom' alone. However, because of the close interplay between them, a full history of each kingdom cannot be written in isolation and a full understanding of the developments of these years is only possible when the histories of the three kingdoms are drawn together into a broader, multiple-kingdom history. In other words, we should be researching and exploring the histories of Ireland, Scotland, and England and Wales, as well as of the Atlantic archipelago as a whole. The wars which rent and reshaped that archipelago in the mid-seventeenth century were Irish, Scottish, English and Welsh, and British. It would be as misleading to ignore the British history and British problems as it would be to deny the separate histories of each of the component kingdoms and to tell only an archipelagic account.

Select bibliography

England and Wales

The best starting point for a general history of seventeenth-century England is Barry Coward, *The Stuart Age* (2nd edn, 1994). On the reign of James I, see Christopher Durston, *James I* (1993) and S.J. Houston, *James I* (2nd edn, 1995), both of which have good bibliographies. On the reign of Charles I down to 1640 a good introduction is Brian Quintrell, *Charles I 1625–1640* (1993), which again has a full bibliography. Quintrell's portrayal of the Personal Rule as a period of mounting if muted discontent is consistent with the findings of more detailed studies and is more convincing than the very favourable view presented by Kevin Sharpe, *The Personal Rule of Charles I* (1992). Various aspects of the early Stuart period are explored in important collections edited by Conrad Russell, *The Origins of the English Civil War* (1973), by Howard Tomlinson, *Before the English Civil War* (1983), and by Richard Cust and Ann Hughes, *Conflict in Early Stuart England* (1989), which has an excellent introduction placing revisionism in a critical context. The best starting point on religion and the church in the pre-war decades is Kenneth Fincham (ed.), *The Early Stuart Church* (1993); here and elsewhere the critical view of Arminianism and of Charles I's religious policies adopted by Fincham, Peter Lake, Nicholas Tyacke and others is more convincing than Peter White's arguments that Charles was merely continuing a well-established policy of enforcing order and uniformity.

The most accessible concise historiographical review of the changing interpretations of the causes of the civil war is Howard Tomlinson's chapter in his own *Before the English Civil War*. The ground is covered in more detail in R.C. Richardson (ed.), *The Debate on the English Revolution Revisited* (1988). Lawrence Stone's wide-ranging *The Causes of the English Revolution* (1972), which incorporates the conclusions from several of his earlier works, remains valuable. Ann Hughes, *The Causes of the English Civil War* (1991) both reviews the historiographical debates of recent decades and presents the author's own interpretation; it has a particularly good and full bibliography. Conrad Russell's *The Causes of the English Civil War* (1990) is a wide-ranging discussion, embracing Scottish and Irish as well as English factors. Many of the arguments have been incorporated within Russell's heavyweight *The Fall of the British Monarchies 1637–42* (1991), though this work has been criticised as being more an English than a truly British account, most notably by John Morrill in an article reprinted as chapter 13 of his *The Nature of the English Revolution* (1993). Morrill's stress upon the centrality of religious convictions and differences as key factors in driving England into civil war is seen in a number of articles reprinted as part one of *The Nature of the English Revolution*. Mark Stoyle's recent works on Devon – *Loyalty and Locality* (1994) – and on Exeter – *From Deliverance to Destruction* (1996) – also underline the importance of religious divisions. David Underdown presents a picture of deeper social and cultural divisions, many of them springing from religion, in *Revel, Riot and Rebellion* (1985). Anthony Fletcher, *The Outbreak of the English Civil War* (1981) explores provincial opinions and pressures in the years 1640–3.

Ivan Roots, *The Great Rebellion* (1966) and Gerald Aylmer, *Rebellion or Revolution?* (1986) give overviews of the period 1640–60. John Kenyon, *The Civil Wars of England* (1988) covers the political and military history of the 1640s. The same period is assessed briefly but clearly by Martyn Bennett, *The English Civil War* (1995), which again spans political and military developments. John Morrill, *The Revolt of the Provinces* (1980) focuses upon the course and impact of the war in the towns and counties of England. This theme and others are explored in two important collections of articles edited by Morrill, *Reactions to the English Civil War* (1982) and *The Impact of the English Civil War* (1991). Charles Carlton, *Going to the Wars* (1992) is a detailed assessment of military life and the military experience. Differing views of the principal parliamentary army are presented by Mark Kishlansky, *The Rise of the New Model Army* (1979), Ian Gentles, *The New Model Army in England, Ireland and Scotland, 1645–53* (1992) and Austin Woolrych, *Soldiers and Statesmen* (1987), which is a masterly account of the army's role in the political manoeuvring of

1647–8. The story is continued by David Underdown, *Pride's Purge* (1971) and by Blair Worden, *The Rump Parliament* (1974). The best introductions to the 1650s are Toby Barnard, *The English Republic* (1982), Austin Woolrych, *England Without a King* (1983) and Ronald Hutton, *The British Republic* (1990), which is the fullest of the three and has a detailed bibliography.

The Welsh experience in the 1640s is covered within a number of broader works, including G.E. Jones, *Modern Wales* (1984), G.H. Jenkins, *The Foundations of Modern Wales* (1987) and Philip Jenkins, *A History of Modern Wales* (1992). Peter Gaunt, *A Nation Under Siege* (1991) focuses upon the experience of the civil wars of 1642–8.

Scotland

Two excellent histories which cover Scotland during this period are Gordon Donaldson, *Scotland: James V to James VII* (1965) and the more recent Keith Brown, *Kingdom or Province? Scotland and the Regal Union, 1603–1715* (1992), which has a good, full bibliography. B.P. Levack focuses on Scotland's relations with England in *The Formation of the British State. England, Scotland and the Union, 1603–1707* (1987). Jenny Wormald, 'James VI and I: two kings or one?', *History* 68 (1983) highlights and questions the differing historical reputations of James as king of Scotland and of England. Different perspectives on the proposed Anglo-Scottish union of the first decade of the seventeenth century are presented by Bruce Galloway, *The Union of England and Scotland, 1603–8* (1986), Neil Cuddy, 'Anglo-Scottish Union and the court of James I, 1603–25', *Transactions of the Royal Historical Society* 5th series, 39 (1989), and Jenny Wormald, 'James VI, James I and the identity of Britain', in Brendan Bradshaw and John Morrill (eds), *The British Problem, c.1534–1707* (1996), which argues that the strongly pro-British sentiments expressed by James in the opening years of his English reign may have been intended merely as an extreme position adopted at the beginning of a bargaining process. Wormald stresses the great differences between England and Scotland and again questions whether James ever really wanted a full union in 'One king, two kingdoms', in Alexander Grant and Keith Stringer (eds), *Uniting the Kingdom?* (1995). John Morrill argues that in religious terms James sought convergence not union in 'A British patriarchy? Ecclesiastical imperialism under the Early Stuarts', in Anthony Fletcher and Peter Roberts (eds), *Religion, Culture and Society in Early Modern Britain* (1994). In the same volume Conrad Russell ranges more widely over the relations between England and Scotland in 'The Anglo-Scottish Union 1603–43: a success?'

The unhappy tale of Charles I's dealings with Scotland is related by a number of recent monographs, notably Maurice Lee, *The Road to Revolution. Scotland under Charles I, 1625–37* (1985), Allan MacInnes, *Charles I and the Making of the Covenanting Movement, 1625–41* (1991), Peter Donald, *An Uncounselled King. Charles I and the Scottish Troubles, 1637–41* (1990) and Mark Fissel, *The Bishops' Wars* (1994). John Morrill (ed.), *The Scottish National Covenant in its British Context* (1990) is an excellent collection, ranging over the causes, making and consequences of the covenant, encompassing the wider British implications and including assessments of the covenanter military experience 1638–51 and Irish-Scottish relations 1638–48 by Edward Furgol and Michael Perceval-Maxwell respectively. Peter Donald, 'New light on the Anglo-Scottish contacts of 1640', *Historical Research* 62 (1989), finds further evidence of clandestine links between Scottish covenanters and some of Charles I's English opponents, a theme pursued by Conrad Russell in *The Fall of the British Monarchies* and in more specialist papers such as 'The Scottish party in English parliaments, 1640–2 or the myth of the English revolution', *Historical Research* 66 (1993).

David Stevenson's work provides the best introduction to the covenanting era. *The Scottish Revolution, 1637–44* (1973) and *Revolution and Counter-Revolution in Scotland, 1644–51* (1977) provide a detailed narrative, *The Government of Scotland Under the Covenanters, 1637–51* (1982) is a collection of documents, and *Scottish Covenanters and Irish Confederates* (1981) explores the interrelationships of the two kingdoms in the mid-seventeenth century. In similar vein, Scotland's military involvement in Ireland is recounted by Raymond Gillespie, 'An army sent from God: Scots at war in Ireland, 1642–9', in N. Macdougall (ed.), *Scotland and War AD 79–1918* (1991). Montrose has attracted several biographers, including John Buchan, *Montrose* (1928) and C.V. Wedgwood, *Montrose* (1952). Cromwell's attitudes to and dealings with Scotland are best introduced by David Stevenson, 'Cromwell, Scotland and Ireland', in John Morrill (ed.), *Oliver Cromwell and the English Revolution* (1990). The fullest account of Scotland after the Cromwellian conquest is F.D. Dow, *Cromwellian Scotland 1651–60* (1979).

Ireland

Several of the works cited in the previous section, such as Stevenson's *Scottish Covenanters and Irish Confederates*, his chapter on 'Cromwell,

Scotland and Ireland', and Gillespie's 'An army sent from God', clearly have as much to say about Ireland as they do about Scotland.

The best general works on Ireland covering this period are probably J.C. Beckett, *The Making of Modern Ireland 1603–1923* (1966) and the more recent Nicholas Canny, *From Reformation to Restoration: Ireland 1534–1660* (1987). However, still the best starting point is T.W. Moody, F.X. Martin and F.J. Byrne (eds), *A New History of Ireland, III. Early Modern Ireland, 1534–1691* (1976); chapters VII–XIII, by Aidan Clarke and Patrick Corish, cover the period 1603–53. Both Ciaran Brady, 'England's defence and Ireland's reform: the dilemma of the Irish viceroys, 1541–1641', in Bradshaw and Morrill (eds), *The British Problem*, and Michael Perceval-Maxwell, 'Ireland and the monarchy in the Early Stuart multiple kingdom', *Historical Journal* 34 (1991) explore Ireland's role within the three nations.

The impact of Wentworth upon Ireland is assessed in different ways by C.V. Wedgwood, *Thomas Wentworth, First Earl of Strafford. A Revaluation* (1961), Hugh Kearney, *Strafford in Ireland, 1633–41* (2nd edn, 1989), Kearney, 'Strafford in Ireland, 1633–40', *History Today* 39 (1989), and Nicholas Canny, 'The attempted anglicization of Ireland in the seventeenth century: an exemplar of "British History" ', in Ronald Asch (ed.), *Three Nations – A Common History?* (1993), which argues that Wentworth harboured dreams, never fulfilled and perhaps not supported by Charles I, of a sweeping Anglicisation of Ireland, involving massive Catholic dispossession and Protestant plantation.

The crisis of 1641 is re-examined by Conrad Russell, 'The British background to the Irish rebellion of 1641', *Historical Research* 61 (1988), Michael Perceval-Maxwell, *The Outbreak of the Irish Rebellion of 1641* (1994), and Brian Mac Cuarta (ed.), *Ulster 1641* (1993). Keith Lindley, 'The impact of the 1641 rebellion upon England and Wales, 1641–5', *Irish Historical Studies* 18 (1972) remains the best, brief assessment of this topic. E.H. Shagon, 'Constructing discord: ideology, propaganda, and English responses to the Irish rebellion of 1641', *Journal of British Studies* 36 (1997), which appeared as this work was going to press, shows how the rebellion further inflamed English politics by locking into existing divisions within the English political elite, different English groupings coming to different conclusions about the nature and causes of the rebellion.

Jane Ohlmeyer, *Civil War and Restoration in Three Stuart Kingdoms. The Career of Randal MacDonnell, the Marquis of Antrim, 1609–83* (1993) is a detailed biography of an important figure of the period, and one who certainly did adopt a British outlook. Ohlmeyer trailed this book with a brief article, 'The Marquis of Antrim: a Stuart turn-kilt?', *History Today* 43 (1993). Ohlmeyer's 'The "Antrim Plot" of 1641 – A Myth?', *Historical Journal* 35 (1992), provoked a debate between her and Michael Perceval-Maxwell in the *Historical Journal* 37 (1994). Another key figure of the 1640s in Ireland is briefly assessed by Andrew Boyd, 'Rinuccini and civil war in Ireland, 1644–9', *History Today* 41 (1991).

Jane Ohlmeyer (ed.), *Ireland from Independence to Occupation, 1641–60* (1995), is an important and impressive collection of new writings on Ireland in the mid-seventeenth century. Particularly useful are Nicholas Canny on the events of 1641, Scott Wheeler on armies and military campaigns in Ireland, and John Adamson on the expansive potential and more limited achievements of Lisle's brief lieutenancy of Ireland, but all the contributions are excellent and relevant. Toby Barnard's piece on 'The Protestant interest, 1641–60', should be read with his 'Crises of identity among Irish Protestants, 1641–85', *Past and Present* 127 (1990). The outcome of the wars in Ireland is explored by K.S. Bottigheimer, *English Money and Irish Land* (1971), and Toby Barnard, *Cromwellian Ireland* (1975).

British history

The recent drive by some historians to adopt a British approach is often traced back to John Pocock's article 'British history: a plea for a new subject', reprinted in *Journal of Modern History* 4 (1975). See also Pocock, 'The limits and divisions of British history', *American History Review* 87 (1982), Steven Ellis, '"Not Mere English": the British perspective 1400–1650', *History Today* 28 (1988), J.C.D. Clark, 'English history's forgotten context: Scotland, Ireland and Wales', *Historical Journal* 32 (1989), and two broad and general histories, R.S. Thompson, *The Atlantic Archipelago: A Political History of the British Isles* (1986) and Hugh Kearney, *The British Isles: A History of the Four Nations* (1989).

The issue of 'multiple kingdoms' has been addressed in various ways by J.H. Elliott, 'The king and the Catalans, 1621–40', *Cambridge Historical Journal* 2 (1955), several contributors, including Elliott, to Mark Greengrass (ed.), *Conquest and Coalescence: The Shaping of the State in Early Modern Europe* (1991), Jenny Wormald, 'The creation of Britain: multiple kingdoms or core and colonies', *Transactions of the Royal Historical Society* 6th series, 2 (1992) and J.H. Elliott, 'A world of composite monarchies', *Past and Present* 137 (1992).

The appearance of Conrad Russell's 'The British problem and the English civil war', *History* 72 (1987), closely followed by further articles and books by Russell with a 'British' perspective, encouraged some historians of the mid-seventeenth century to focus on British rather than purely English issues, as reflected in many of the recent articles and papers already cited. Several edited collections on the same theme have appeared during the 1990s, four of which are either devoted to the early modern period or contain substantial sections exploring the sixteenth and seventeenth centuries.

Part 2 of Ronald Asch (ed.), *Three Nations – A Common History?* comprises three papers on the theme 'The war of the three kingdoms and the British problem in the 17th century'. Nicholas Canny's paper on 'The attempted anglicization of Ireland in the seventeenth century' has already been mentioned for his assessment of Wentworth in Ireland, but he begins more generally by criticising 'British history' as overly narrow and often unbalanced. John Morrill, 'The Britishness of the English revolution', is a wide-ranging defence of a 'British' approach, though acknowledging that each of the three kingdoms experienced war in different ways and to different extents. Keith Brown, 'British history: a sceptical comment', again criticises the approach as too narrow and argues that few participants in the wars had a truly British outlook, the Scots (and to a lesser extent the Irish) instead working for a federalist settlement as the best way to preserve nationalist objectives. The first half of Asch's introduction to the volume also focuses on the relationship between the three kingdoms in the Stuart period.

Part 3 of Alexander Grant and Keith Stringer (eds), *Uniting the Kingdom?* (1995) comprises five papers on the theme 'Building the early modern state'. Of the papers relevant to the seventeenth century, Jenny Wormald's on James VI and I has already been cited. Conrad Russell's wide-ranging 'Composite monarchies in early modern Europe: the British and Irish example' notes the continuing differences between the three kingdoms in the Early Stuart period, and John Morrill's equally broad 'Three kingdoms and one commonwealth? The enigma of mid-seventeenth-century Britain and Ireland' highlights the continuing uncertainty and ambiguity over the relationship between the three kingdoms during the 1640s while also following John Pocock in stressing that each kingdom endured a distinctive form of war during the mid-seventeenth century, different from that suffered by its two neighbours. Nicholas Canny's 'Irish, Scottish and Welsh responses to centralisation, c.1530–c.1640: a comparative perspective' is unusually critical of James I's handling of Ireland; a self-proclaimed 'Brito-sceptic', Canny also takes the opportunity to criticise British history and argues in favour of a simpler comparative approach. In an important introductory chapter,

'British history as a "New Subject": politics, perspectives and prospects', David Cannadine traces how and why the new approach has come about and assesses the strengths and weaknesses of 'British history', highlighting the dangers.

Several contributions to Steven Ellis and Sarah Barber (eds), *Conquest and Union. Fashioning a British State, 1485–1725* (1995) are pertinent, including Ellis's brief introduction to 'The concept of British history' and John Morrill's chapter on 'The fashioning of Britain', which explores multiple kingdoms, the Anglo-Scottish union and the churches of the three kingdoms. Keith Brown, 'The origins of a British aristocracy: integration and its limitations before the treaty of union', develops an argument rehearsed in several earlier articles, that the Scottish aristocracy retained a strong and distinctive national identity and culture long after 1603. Sarah Barber, 'Scotland and Ireland under the commonwealth: a question of loyalty', looks at republican views of the relationship between the three kingdoms both in the 1640s and after the establishment of the republican regime in England in 1649.

Several contributions to the fourth 'British' collection, Brendan Bradshaw and John Morrill (eds), *The British Problem, c.1534–1707* (1996), have already been cited, notably Jenny Wormald on James VI and I, and Ciaran Brady on Irish viceroys. Although most chapters have some bearing upon the early and mid-seventeenth century, two others are particularly relevant here. John Pocock, 'The Atlantic archipelago and the war of the three kingdoms', both defends the 'British' approach and notes its limitations, stressing that each kingdom retained its own distinctive history, no matter how much it converged, collided or interacted with those of its neighbours, and highlighting that each of the three kingdoms suffered a different and distinctive type of war in the mid-seventeenth century. The paper by Derek Hirst, 'The English republic and the meaning of Britain', originally published in the *Journal of Modern History* 66 (1994) and reprinted here, explores the theory and practice of the union of Ireland and Scotland with and under England in the 1650s and explores the British union which emerged from the British wars.